Virtual Training Basics

Cindy Huggett

ASTD
PRESS

Alexandria, Virginia

Credit Information
Images in this book are reprinted with permission from Adobe Systems Incorporated. © 2010 Adobe Systems Incorporated. All rights reserved.
Adobe® Acrobat® Connect™ Pro is a product of Adobe, the Adobe logo, Acrobat, Acrobat Connect, and Flash are either registered trademarks or trademarks of Adobe Systems Incorporated in the United States and/or other countries.

Images in this book are reprinted with permission from Microsoft Corporation. © 2010 Microsoft Corporation. All rights reserved.
Microsoft® Excel®, PowerPoint®, and Windows® are either registered trademarks or trademarks of Microsoft Corporation in the United States and/or other countries.

ASTD Press is an internationally renowned source of insightful and practical information on workplace learning and performance topics, including training basics, evaluation and return on investment, instructional systems development, e-learning, leadership, and career development. Visit us at www.astd.org/astdpress.

Ordering information: Books published by ASTD Press can be purchased by visiting our website at store.astd.org or by calling 800.628.2783 or 703.683.8100.

Library of Congress Control Number: 2009903732

ISBN-10: 1-56286-702-4
ISBN-13: 978-1-56286-702-7

ASTD Press Editorial Staff:
Director of Content: Dean Smith
Manager, ASTD Press: Jacqueline Edlund-Braun
Senior Associate Editor: Tora Estep
Senior Associate Editor: Justin Brusino
Senior Associate Editor: Victoria DeVaux

Editorial, Design, and Production: Abella Publishing Services, LLC
Cover Design: Steve Fife

Printed by Sheridan Books, Inc., Chelsea, MI, www.sheridanbooks.com

Contents

About the
Training Basics Series

A STD's *Training Basics* series recognizes and, in some ways, celebrates the fast-paced, ever-changing reality of organizations today. Jobs, roles, and expectations change quickly. One day you might be a network administrator or a process line manager, and the next day you might be asked to train 50 employees in basic computer skills or to instruct line workers in quality processes.

Where do you turn for help? The ASTD *Training Basics* series is designed to be your one-stop solution. The series takes a minimalist approach to your learning curve dilemma and presents only the information you need to be successful. Each book in the series guides you through key aspects of training: giving presentations, making the transition to the role of trainer, designing and delivering training, and evaluating training. The books in the series also include some advanced skills such as performance and basic business proficiencies.

The ASTD *Training Basics* series is the perfect tool for training and performance professionals looking for easy-to-understand materials that will prepare non-trainers to take on a training role. In addition, this series is the perfect reference tool for any trainer's bookshelf and a quick way to hone your existing skills.

Foreword

Only Perfect Practice Makes Perfect

The concept of e-learning in many formats has been around since 1997, as Cindy aptly describes in her first chapter. Age, however, isn't a precursor for maturity, and repetition isn't a synonym for expertise.

So while the training profession is moving into its second decade of "practicing" the concept of e-learning, and more specifically virtual learning, few of us have been "perfecting" our design and delivery. As Vince Lombardi said, "Practice does not make perfect. Only perfect practice makes perfect." Cindy gives us the tools in this book to begin to *perfect* our virtual training skills.

Why is this important? Most organizations are seeing an increase in the use of virtual training. Travel restrictions, budget cuts, and an increasingly technology-savvy workforce have led most organizations to rethink how they continue to meet the learning needs of their employees. Organizations are asking their trainers to deliver more content online. Trainers are expected to have the skills to design and deliver virtual training.

Unfortunately, the concept of virtual learning is still not very well understood by either organizations or practitioners. Virtual training often falls short of the quality standards expected in traditional settings. Most of these instances are due to a lack of appropriate design and limited knowledge of the skill variations required. It seems that many are still under the misperception that virtual training is simply classroom training set to a different tune. Although almost anything can be taught virtually, those who design and deliver training have not always attended to the translation considerations for both the material and the delivery skills required. Cindy addresses these differences in a way that every reader will understand.

Too often I pick up a book about technology that is way over my head. I may be lost while reading the first chapter! The most unique aspect of this book is that it doesn't assume the reader knows anything about virtual training. It starts with the basics, including definitions and explanations of the necessary hardware and software. It walks us through every aspect of virtual training, from how to set up for a class, to what the trainer needs to know about technology, to what to do when everything goes wrong.

Cindy convinces us that virtual training is "still training" and requires us to tap into all the good things we do in the classroom. And she takes it one step further. She addresses the differences between classroom and virtual training, providing techniques to address the differences. Not only is this practical, but it gives us a calming sense of "I can do that!"

I remember the first virtual training that I conducted. It took me quite some time after it was over to realize that I had treated the session differently. I had thrown out many of the basics of good training, such as facilitating discussion and engaging participants, just because the participants were not in the same room with me. One of the greatest concerns for trainers is that they cannot "see" the participants. One of the most valuable aspects of this book is that Cindy describes other methods of "observing" participants that are available to the virtual trainer. There are ways to "see" your participants. I sure wish I had read this book before my first virtual training session!

Throughout the book, Cindy combines her experience with the experience of other training colleagues. She uses other virtual trainers' quotes to share tips and lessons learned. What I loved about these quotes is that they often present varying views. So even if her colleagues have a different approach from Cindy's, she presents both sides and allows readers to select what will work best for them. The 10 steps in this guide will prepare you better than any other book I've read for your role as a virtual trainer.

If you are searching for professional development that is practical, enabling you to put it to use immediately, you have found the right book. Spend the weekend reading and you'll be a more knowledgeable virtual trainer by Monday. The book is chock full of worksheets, activities, basic rules, assessments, and checklists that ensure ease of understanding and implementing the concepts.

Here's a sample of the topics I found most helpful to perfect my virtual training skills:

- managing your virtual classroom time
- engaging participants in the virtual classroom
- juggling all the elements of virtual training and advice for multitasking
- asking well-thought-out questions
- giving instructions for group activities
- using your voice and speaking skills to enhance the participants' learning.

Cindy personalizes each of the topics through stories that illustrate her advice, making your learning come alive. You will feel as if she is writing directly to you when she asks a question you've been thinking about or when she highlights one of her slipups that matches one of your fears. This is Cindy's way of telling us that she has been there, too. She illuminates our learning by taking us by the hand and walking us through each of the concepts in her reassuring way.

The best reason for any product is to fill a need and Cindy has done that with this book. I don't think there is anything on the market that hits the mark quite like *Virtual Training Basics*. Cindy is an early adopter of technology, starting her training career as a software instructor. She has delivered hundreds of virtual training classes for more than a decade. She is passionate about developing trainers and helping them be the best that they can be. Who better to coach all of us to be better virtual trainers? You are in good hands with this book by your side and Cindy as your guide to *perfect* your virtual training skills.

Elaine Biech
Author of *ASTD's Ultimate Train the Trainer*

Preface

■ ■

So you've been asked to deliver training in a virtual classroom, and you don't know where to begin. Or you've delivered a few online classes, and are not quite comfortable with the technology. Or maybe you keep hearing that virtual training is the wave of the future and you want to stay current. If any of these scenarios describe you—congratulations! You've come to the right place.

This book will help you get started in the process of delivering successful virtual classes. It is designed for classroom trainers who are migrating to virtual delivery. This book will also help first-time virtual trainers, and anyone who is asked to present or facilitate online.

The Move to Virtual Training

Over the past decade, industry studies have shown a trend toward increased virtual training. The *2009 ASTD State of the Industry Report* indicated that instructor-led online learning increased from 4.24 percent of overall formal learning hours delivered in 2006 to 6.42 percent in 2007. While this increase may not seem like much, that's an increase of over 2 percent in one year! And when you consider that the annual total dollar amount spent by U.S. organizations on employee learning and development is estimated at $134.07 billion, we're talking about a significant yearly increase in virtual training delivery.

More recent research by Bersin & Associates in *The Corporate Learning Factbook 2009* indicates that average training expenditures decreased in 2008 because of the economic downturn. Bersin also reports a reduction in virtual classroom training, mostly as a result of budget and staffing cuts.

While the full impact of this spending reduction is not yet fully known, another interesting 2009 ASTD research report, *Learning in Tough Economic Times*, found that nearly seven out of 10 respondents are "looking for ways to become more efficient at delivering learning" and "more than half had restricted travel for learners." The survey respondents indicated interest in "new and less expensive methods of delivering learning, including e-learning, simulations, and other online options."

While virtual instructor-led training is not the only online option available, it still represents a significant portion of training delivered to learners. More and more trainers will be asked to use technology in training implementations. Traditional classroom training is not going away; however, training professionals must diversify their skill set in order to stay relevant in the new economy.

Just because a trainer is effective in a traditional training class does not mean he or she will be effective in the virtual classroom. It is a new delivery environment. Many trainers—especially those who are not technology savvy—need to learn the nuances of the online classroom. Virtual training delivery requires an updated skill set for trainers.

This book will help both new and experienced classroom trainers get started in the virtual classroom.

> We'll look at our definition of virtual training in more depth throughout the chapters; however, this book defines virtual training as a **synchronous** online event, with participants and a trainer meeting together at the same time, using a software program designed as a virtual classroom.

Why This Book?

When I talked with fellow trainers about virtual training, the question was always the same: "How did you learn?" Which really meant they wanted to know, "How can I learn?" After having this same conversation over and over, it became apparent to me that a basic "how-to" book was needed for those brand-new to virtual training. A resource to answer the questions:

▶ Where should you start when learning how to deliver in the virtual classroom?
▶ How do you learn to deliver in the virtual classroom?
▶ What's different about virtual training as compared to classroom training?

This book seeks to answer those questions. It represents my experience in delivering hundreds of virtual classes over the years. It also contains advice and stories from my training colleagues. We hope you can learn from our consolidated experiences, and hope it leads you toward becoming an effective virtual trainer.

Although this book is primarily written for classroom trainers who are new to virtual training, anyone needing to lead virtual meetings will benefit from the tips found in it. In addition, trainers with limited experience in the online classroom may also discover new tips and techniques that will benefit them.

Format of the Book

This book is divided into 10 chapters. They can be seen as the 10 steps you should follow to become a great virtual trainer. Each chapter outlines a necessary skill or preparation step for effective online delivery.

While I recommend you read and apply all of the steps outlined in this book, if you are short on time, just look at the beginning and ending of each chapter for the basics. It's also OK to jump to the chapter you need, especially if you have done this for a while or just need help with a specific topic. You will find this book is full of checklists and worksheets to get you up to speed quickly.

By the way, because successful virtual training promotes networking and collaboration, I asked several of my friends and colleagues to offer advice, tips, and share stories of their own. I think you'll enjoy learning from their experience in addition to my own.

Organization of the Chapters

This book is presented in chapters that are loosely organized in the order you should follow them. I say "loosely" because many of them occur simultaneously when you are delivering a virtual class. For example, "Harness Your Voice" in chapter 7 and "Engage Your Participants" in chapter 8 both happen during delivery. Some of the steps need to be done prior to the class, such as "Set Up for Success" in chapter 5 and "Practice, Practice, Practice" in chapter 9. As I've already mentioned, it is OK for you to go directly to the chapter where you need help, or to skip around the book in the order that makes sense to you.

Here is a brief overview of the chapters:

Chapter 1: What Is Virtual Training? There are varying definitions of virtual training, and it's important to know the options available to you as a training professional. In this chapter, we'll define what "virtual training" is, and what it isn't.

Chapter 2: Virtual Training Is Still Training. What's similar between face-to-face classroom training and virtual training? It's still about training! Improving productivity and getting better business results are still the goals. Technology is just a tool to get us there. You can rest assured that training skills are still needed in the virtual classroom. In this chapter, we'll review the training skills needed to be a successful virtual facilitator.

Chapter 3: Learn About Technology. To be an effective virtual trainer, you need to be 100 percent comfortable with your computer, both its hardware and software. You'll also need basic technical troubleshooting skills. In this chapter, we'll focus on the technology background you need when training in the online classroom.

Chapter 4: Master Virtual Classroom Software Programs. Just like a craftsman masters the tools of his trade, a virtual trainer must expertly know the software programs used in online delivery. In this chapter, we'll cover the typical capabilities of virtual classroom software and how to use its features in an online class.

Chapter 5: Set Up for Success. What a trainer does prior to class affects the success of the class. A virtual trainer's preparation includes learning the content and learning about the participants, as well as setting up the classroom. In this chapter, we'll go through a recommended preparation process, starting with your initial look at the material through getting ready for a virtual class.

Chapter 6: Get Really Good at Multitasking. Virtual trainers need to talk, type, and click at the same time, juggling the course material, technology, and participants all at once. In this chapter, we'll review 10 tips to be a better multitasker.

Chapter 7: Harness Your Voice. In the virtual classroom, trainers connect with participants using their voice. In this chapter, we'll consider ways to use your voice—and how not to use it—so that it's an asset to your virtual delivery style.

Chapter 8: Engage Your Participants. Trainers must engage participants in any class, and even more so in the virtual classroom. In this chapter, we'll learn how to get participants' attention and keep them involved throughout a virtual class.

Chapter 9: Practice, Practice, Practice. Any time you learn a new skill, practice makes perfect. This is true with virtual training as well. While you may never be "perfect" in the classroom, you will gain confidence and experience when you practice. In this chapter, we'll review tips for getting practice, and ways to get quality feedback to improve your delivery.

Chapter 10: Know What to Do When Everything Goes Wrong. Virtual trainers can and should expect technical challenges. In this chapter, we'll cover what types of things typically go wrong in the online classroom, and what you should do when these problems happen.

Look for These Icons

What's Inside This Chapter

Each chapter opens with a summary of the topics addressed in the chapter. You can use this reference to find the areas that interest you most.

Think About This

These are helpful tips for how to use the tools and techniques presented in the chapter.

Basic Rules

These rules cut to the chase. They represent important concepts and assumptions that form the foundation of virtual training.

Noted

This icon calls out additional information.

Getting It Done

The final section of each chapter supports your ability to take the content of that chapter and apply it to your situation. Sometimes this section contains a list of questions for you to ponder. Sometimes it is a self-assessment tool. And sometimes it is a list of action steps you can take to enhance your facilitation.

Acknowledgments

I dedicate this book to my best friend and husband, Bobby Huggett. Without his love and support, this book would never have been written. I also want to honor my grandmother, Martha Leeson, for her encouragement along the way.

I give special thanks to the training professionals who willingly shared their advice and stories about the virtual classroom: Mike Abrams, Lynne Hobbs, Kella Price, Kathy Shurte, Tracy Stallard, Jeff Smith, Rebecca Ward, Jim Wilcox, Joe Willmore, and Sharon Wingron. I am grateful to each one of you for your willingness to offer your wisdom. Your contributions have enriched this book. Thank you.

I also express my gratitude to Wendy Gates Corbett, my *Infoline* co-author and friend, for sharing her thoughts, suggestions, and insights on the content, as well as her virtual training expertise.

Finally, thank you to Paige Smith for reading an early version of this manuscript, and to Justin Brusino at ASTD Press for his patience, encouragement, and advice.

Cindy Huggett
Psalm 115:1
May 2010

1

What Is
Virtual Training?

··

What's Inside This Chapter

In this chapter, you'll learn

▶ Common terms associated with virtual training
▶ Guidelines for moving from traditional to virtual training
▶ What virtual training looks like
▶ How to determine if virtual training is the right solution.

If you ask 10 different trainers to define "virtual training," you will probably get 10 different responses. To one person it might be taking a self-paced e-learning course, and to another it might mean a Second Life meeting. Virtual training is a broad term with many different interpretations.

In some ways, it's like the word *health*. When you tell someone that you want to "get healthy," they might think you will be changing your eating habits. To someone else it might mean exercising, getting more sleep, or losing weight. Health is a multi-faceted word. It could mean any of those things or more, depending upon its context and who is talking about it. In reality, the full scope of the word *health* encompasses all aspects of a person's well-being: physical, social, emotional, and spiritual. Yet when people talk about their health, they are usually referring to just one specific aspect of it. It's the same with virtual training. Virtual training is multifaceted, and could mean many things depending upon its context and who is talking about it.

Because this book's definition of virtual training might not be your definition of virtual training, let's spend some time clarifying various elements of it and defining some terms.

Starting With the Basics

Training classes help people learn new skills. "Traditional" training classes have pre-defined learning objectives, are held at a set time and place, and are taught by a trainer. Participants register for the class, show up at the pre-assigned time, and leave with new knowledge and skills ready to be applied back on the job.

These traditional training classes vary in style, length, and format. They may be highly participatory or they could be lecture-based. The class size may be small enough for intimate discussion around a table or large enough to fill an auditorium. The class may be two hours or two days in length. It may be contained in one short meeting or it may span several months.

Virtual training has the same types of options. It can vary in style, length, and format.

The most common terms associated with virtual training include

- online learning
- e-learning
- synchronous
- asynchronous
- webcast
- webinar
- Web 2.0
- informal learning
- blended learning
- virtual instructor-led training (vILT).

Let's review each one in context, so that we can establish the boundaries for our definition of virtual training.

Noted

There are a lot of things called virtual training.
—Joe Willmore, President and Founder, Willmore Consulting Group

Online Learning? E-Learning? When personal computers were introduced into the workplace and our daily lives, we used them to automate processes and simplify routines. It was natural for training to follow. Trainers began looking for ways to automate learning, and traditional training moved onto the computer.

At first it was called "electronic learning," or *e-learning* for short, because it was learning via computer. The term e-learning has evolved to refer to any type of training that requires a computer. Some people use the hyphenated spelling "e-learning" while others run it together "eLearning." Both versions are widely accepted.

After the introduction of the Internet and web browsers, trainers took advantage of this new technology. When you accessed training via the Internet, it was called *online learning.* This term has also evolved to refer to any type of training that requires a computer, whether the Internet is involved or not.

Many people consider online learning and e-learning to be the same thing. Online learning naturally requires a computer and therefore uses electronic tools. However, you can distinguish between online learning and e-learning by looking at the learners' interaction. It's a very subtle yet important distinction.

Some online learning is self-paced, completed individually without any interaction with others. However, most types of online learning occur in conjunction with other learners. Learners collaborate with each other and with a trainer. *Online learning is an umbrella term that refers to all types of interactive training that uses an Internet-connected computer.*

On the other hand, e-learning more commonly refers *only* to self-paced individual training. Participants taking an e-learning course would log in to a website and complete an assignment on their own. There is usually no interaction with other learners, or with a trainer. While the e-learning course uses a website, it is distinguished by its individual nature. See Table 1–1 for more information.

Table 1–1. Distinguishing Between E-Learning and Online Learning

	e-learning	online learning
Requires a computer	Yes	Yes
Requires Internet access	Not necessary, but sometimes used	Yes
Interact with other learners	Self-paced, interacting with computer only	Yes

Virtual training requires a computer with Internet access and has interactivity between the learners and a trainer. Therefore, throughout this book I will use the terms "virtual training" and "online training" interchangeably.

Synchronous Versus Asynchronous. Synchronous and asynchronous refer to the meeting time of the training. In a synchronous training event, the participants and trainer meet together at a set day and time. Synchronous training events usually use an Internet-based software program specifically created to host online meetings, events, and training.

A participant in a synchronous training class would receive a welcome announcement such as: *Class begins at 9 a.m. Eastern Time on Thursday, August 20. See below for location information and directions for accessing the room.*

In asynchronous training, the participants and trainer do not meet together at the same time. Asynchronous refers to self-paced learning that occurs over time as the participants' schedules allow. Common tools used in an online asynchronous training event include threaded discussion boards, email messages, podcasts, and wikis.

A participant in an asynchronous training class would receive a welcome announcement that might say this: *Sometime before Friday, August 14, log on to our class website discussion board and post an introduction. Your first class assignment will be due by Thursday, August 20. Send an email to your trainer with any questions or concerns.*

Both synchronous and asynchronous training events usually include opportunities for collaboration and interaction between participants. In a synchronous event, the collaboration happens together in real time, and in asynchronous training the collaboration occurs intermittently over time. The two main differences between them are the software tools used to conduct the training and the timing of the events.

This book's definition of virtual training applies to synchronous online events only.

Face-to-Face Training Versus Virtual Training. When the participants are together with the trainer in the same room, it's called in-person or face-to-face training (sometimes abbreviated f2f). When participants are separated by distance and meet online, it's called virtual training.

Virtual training can be audio-only by conference call. A training colleague recently told me that one of his clients wanted to do "virtual training." He assumed they meant an online synchronous delivery, only to find out they simply meant training via conference call. However, most virtual training also includes a visual connection via a shared website or collaboration software program.

Some might consider *video conferencing* to be a type of virtual training. Participants are separated by distance yet are able to see one another on a video screen. Video conferencing systems are typically located in corporate boardrooms. One distinguishing factor between video conferencing and virtual training is the audio-visual technology required to make a video conference happen. In addition, video conferencing usually has a group of people gathered around the board room screen, while virtual training has only one person per online connection.

The type of virtual training covered in this book does not include video conferencing. Virtual training may or may not include video, and instead uses a computer's Internet connection and web browser to connect to a virtual classroom software platform.

Online Presentations, Meetings, and Webcasts. An online presentation, sometimes called a webcast, could be compared to an in-person seminar. In this type of seminar, a presenter speaks to the attendees. There is little interaction between the presenter and participants, except for possible Q&A opportunities during the program.

I recently attended a webcast sponsored by a well-known financial institution. At the designated start time, I logged on to a website and saw the speakers and their presentation slides. I estimate there were at least a thousand other participants logged in as well. There was limited interaction between the speakers and attendees, except for the ability for attendees to submit questions electronically. The speakers addressed a few of the questions during the program, but the rest went unanswered. While it was an expertly produced, informative webcast, I would not consider it to be virtual training.

If we had met face to face instead of online, this webcast would probably have been called a *meeting*. It would have been held in a large auditorium, with the speakers on stage behind a podium and screens hanging overhead to display the visual aids.

While it is possible to create limited interactivity in this type of event, it's mostly just a talking head who is sharing information. This is not considered training in a face-to-face environment, and therefore would not be considered training in the virtual environment. A webcast is not training.

While many of the tips contained in this book will help you be more effective at leading webcasts and online meetings, our focus is specifically on virtual training.

Webinars and Virtual Training. Most people use the terms webinars and virtual training interchangeably. The word webinar sounds like seminar, and it has become the word du jour for synchronous online training.

While most people do not distinguish between webinars and virtual instructor-led training, in my experience they have different intended outcomes and therefore are not the same thing. The goal of a webinar is to impart knowledge, while the goal of virtual training is to improve performance. This difference may seem slight, but it is significant enough to warrant discussion.

Webinars raise participant awareness of a topic. They are used to impart information to the attendees. For example, if a corporate human resources department needed to share information with employees about an upcoming annual benefit enrollment period, it may choose to share that information via webinar. This webinar could include interactivity, with polling questions and chat, but it would not be considered a training class. While webinars may have two-way communications between presenter and participants, they may or may not ultimately result in the participants' behavior change or have an impact on participants' performance after the event. Webinars are simply an online opportunity to interactively share information.

Webinars are helpful and useful in the right context. They have their place and purpose. There are times when participants simply need awareness of new information, and interactivity will help communicate it. Most of the tips covered in this book will be as useful to a webinar facilitator as to a trainer leading a virtual class.

Think About This

A *webinar* differs from a *webcast* in two ways.

First, a webcast usually has a very large audience. The attendees stay anonymous and usually cannot see one another online because the attendee list is hidden from view. Alternatively, webinars could have any size audience.

Second, a webcast has little, if any, interactivity. It's designed for one-way communication from the presenter to the attendees. Conversely, a webinar may have some interactivity built into its design. Webinars are always more engaging than webcasts.

A virtual training class is different from a webinar because it has predefined learning objectives. These objectives are tied to performance outcomes. And ideally, these performance outcomes will have positive impact on business results. During a virtual training class, the trainer will check for knowledge transfer. In addition, participants have an opportunity to practice and apply their new skills.

Even though *webinar* is a popular term and many people use it to describe virtual training, this book will distinguish between them and focus on virtual training.

Think About This

Webinar and *webcast* are popular terms and many people use them to describe virtual training interchangeably. Therefore, ask about the intended outcome of the event so that you share a common understanding.

Refer to Table 1–2 to help you distinguish between a webcast, a webinar, and virtual training.

Table 1–2. Differences Between a Webcast, a Webinar, and Virtual Training

	Webcast	Webinar	Virtual Training
Relative size of audience	Large	Any size	Small
Interactivity?	No	Yes	Yes
Pre-defined performance-based learning objectives?	No	Usually not	Yes
Face-to-face equivalent	Presentation or meeting	Seminar	Training class

Blended Learning. When a training class combines multiple delivery methods, it's considered blended learning. A blended learning solution might include a mix of traditional face-to-face classes, coaching, and participation in a discussion board. Or, it could be a series of synchronous online training events with self-paced assignments in between. Even assigning a prereading before coming to class could be considered blended learning. It is a "blend" of various activities to achieve a learning outcome.

Blended learning usually takes place over a period of time—several weeks or even several months. For instance, if a new employee orientation program took place in a blended format, it might look like this: Employees receive a packet in the mail containing materials to read prior to class. They are directed to log on to a website and post an introduction message on the company's new hire discussion board. On their first day of work, they attend a face-to-face instructor led class. Afterward, they are given two homework assignments to complete. The total completion of these activities makes up the overall blended new hire orientation.

Many years ago, I facilitated a leadership class for a group of managers who were dispersed in many locations. I used a blended format for the program. It spanned six months and included a series of self-paced e-learning courses with assignments in between. In addition, we met every three weeks in a synchronous virtual classroom so the managers could collaborate together to practice new skills and compare their notes. By the end of the program, the managers had completed approximately 26 hours of training through the various activities.

Virtual training is frequently one component of a larger blended learning curriculum.

Web 2.0. The Internet was originally called the "World Wide Web" because it allowed computers to connect to each other in patterns reminiscent of a spider web (notice the "www" at the beginning of most Internet addresses). It was commonly referred to in its abbreviated form, "the web."

Even though the underlying technology of the Internet has not changed much since its inception, the way we use the Internet has evolved over time. In the early 2000s, as functionality increased and Internet usage spread, people started sharing content and interacting with one another. Websites and programs that allowed this type of user-generated content became known as the second generation of Internet, or *Web 2.0*. Internet sites like MySpace, Facebook, Twitter, and YouTube allow users to share content and comment on each other's posts. Because of their collaboration and information sharing properties, Web 2.0 programs are a fertile source of learning possibilities.

One program in particular—Second Life—stands out in the discussion of virtual training. Second Life combines user-generated content with a three-dimensional virtual world. It allows users to connect in unprecedented ways. Some organizations are using Second Life to conduct virtual face-to-face training classes. There is no shortage of learning opportunities in Second Life.

While Web 2.0 and Second Life have significant implications for the future of the training industry, their technology is beyond the scope of what we'll focus on in this book. Our definition of virtual training will only cover the synchronous online classroom.

Informal Learning. Much of what is learned by someone actually takes place outside of the formal classroom. This is called informal learning. Informal learning can be on-the-job training where someone learns by doing. It can also be reading a book or asking a colleague for assistance. Most informal learning is not captured or recorded as training. It simply happens out of necessity.

Marcia Conner, an expert in informal learning, estimates that "informal learning accounts for over 75 percent of the learning taking place in organizations today." Informal learning finds its way into our vocabulary related to virtual training because of its relationship to Web 2.0. Much informal learning takes place over the web as learners visit websites and collaborate with one another.

For example, I recently needed to learn about digital audio recording devices. I searched the web for information and learned a little about them in the process. I also found a Twitter post (called a "tweet") about a recording device, and contacted the person who wrote it. He recommended one of his colleagues with expertise in these types of devices, so I followed up with that person. We connected first by Twitter and then by telephone. Through these connections, I learned enough about the devices to complete the task I needed to do without ever participating in a formal training event.

Once again, informal learning should be on the minds of trainers who are paying attention to trends in the workplace learning and performance industry. Informal learning significantly influences organizational knowledge and employee performance. However, informal learning is beyond the scope of what we'll focus on in this book. Our definition of virtual training will stay in the synchronous online classroom.

Virtual Training. So, what is virtual training? Virtual training occurs as a synchronous online event, with participants and a trainer meeting together at the same time. Because a training professional facilitates the event, it is sometimes called virtual instructor-led training (vILT).

Virtual training uses a software program specifically designed for real-time collaboration on the web. This software application is called a virtual classroom. Some common virtual classroom programs are

- ▶ Cisco WebEx Training Center
- ▶ Adobe Acrobat Connect Pro
- ▶ Microsoft Office Live Meeting
- ▶ Citrix GoToWebinar
- ▶ Elluminate Live!

We'll cover the intricacies of virtual classroom programs in chapter 4.

Virtual training can be a one-time event or part of a blended learning solution. It has learning objectives and performance-driven outcomes. The participants attend to acquire new knowledge, close a performance gap, and practice new skills.

Remember, virtual training is not a meeting held via videoconference. Nor is it a webcast or a self-paced web course. Virtual training is also not traditional classroom training transferred to the web. It has more nuances than a face-to-face class and a different set of interaction dynamics.

Virtual training is a *synchronous* online event, with participants and a trainer meeting together at the same time, using a software program designed as a virtual classroom.

Basic Rule 1

The term *virtual training* has many meanings. When discussing virtual training with someone, ensure you have a common definition. Ask questions to understand what they mean when they say virtual training.

Moving from Traditional to Virtual Training

If you are asked to take the material from a physical classroom training course and deliver it in the online classroom, be cautious! It's not a one-to-one translation. One minute of classroom time does not equal one minute of virtual classroom time. Some face-to-face activities simply don't translate or even make sense online.

This is not a book on instructional design for virtual training. However, trainers are frequently asked to conduct their face-to-face classes in the synchronous virtual classroom. In most cases, a traditional training class does not translate word for word into the online environment.

If you need to turn a traditional class to a virtual one, follow these three basic guidelines for success:

1. *Begin with the learning objectives.* Go back to the training class' original design documents and review the performance outcomes. What should learners know or do as a result of participating in the class? Establish these as the groundwork for your virtual training.
2. *Determine the overall format that could achieve this outcome.* Consider creating a blended solution with a mixture of methods. Ask yourself: What activities could you ask the learners do on their own versus what should be done together virtually?

3. *Take the opportunity to re-create the training from scratch.* Use activity ideas from the classroom content, and make full use of the virtual classroom software tools available to engage participants in the learning.

See Table 1–3 for a comparison between a traditional face-to-face class and a synchronous virtual training class.

What Virtual Training Looks Like

When I describe virtual training to people not familiar with it, it's hard for them to visualize the experience. Here's a quick snapshot:

Michelle is a trainer for a large telecommunications company. She's located in Cincinnati, Ohio. She schedules a 90-minute virtual class for Thursday at 11 a.m. Eastern time. About a week prior to the training date, she sends an email message with directions and logistics to her participants. About an hour prior to the start time, she sits at her office desk, logs in to the virtual classroom software, and gets ready for the event. She uploads her Microsoft Office PowerPoint presentation file, opens the first polling question, and prepares the virtual whiteboard. She completes all of her preclass preparation and waits for everyone to arrive.

Table 1–3. Differences Between Face-to-Face and Virtual Training

	Traditional face to face	Synchronous virtual
Based on learning objectives and performance outcomes	✓	✓
Participants and the trainer meet together at the same time	✓	✓
Participants are dispersed in various geographic locations during the event		✓
Participants connect to the class via computer with Internet connection		✓
Can be part of a blended learning solution	✓	✓

Around 10:50 a.m., the participants start entering the classroom. They do this from the comfort of their own respective offices: sitting at their own desks, opening up their Internet browsers, and clicking on the link from Michelle's email message.

One participant, Moira, is in her office in Dallas, Texas. She clicks on the link and goes straight to the log in page. She types in her name and email address, and waits for the classroom software to load on her screen. While waiting, she dials the telephone number found in Michelle's email message, and enters the conference call passcode when prompted. Moira hears Michelle's voice on the line, and says hello to greet her. The other participants follow the same steps to join the class.

The participants are able to see what Michelle has prepared for them on the screen. They see the names of the other attendees, a PowerPoint slide, and a chat window.

The participants communicate with each other verbally and online through typing in the chat window. Throughout the class, Michelle asks them to respond to poll questions, write on the screen for input, and participate in activities. At one point, Michelle assigns the participants into virtual breakout groups, and Moira is able to talk privately with her partner, Julie. They practice one of the new skills before returning to the large group for discussion.

By 12:30 p.m., class finishes, and Michelle asks everyone to complete a follow-up assignment to apply what they've just learned.

Figure 1–1. Sample Virtual Training Classroom Using Adobe Acrobat Connect Pro

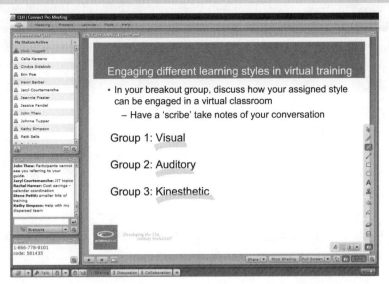

Source: Adobe® product screenshot reprinted with permission from Adobe Systems Incorporated

As you can see, there seem to be many similarities between a virtual class and a face-to-face one. Each class is scheduled for a specific time, and participants are engaged through activities and exercises. However, no participants in a virtual session actually leave their workspace to attend, and they cannot see one another during class. Also, virtual classes tend to be shorter in length than their face-to-face counterparts.

Keep in mind that not every virtual training class is exactly like the one previously described. This story simply illustrates a typical experience for the trainer and participants.

Determining if Going Virtual Is the Right Solution

As mentioned earlier, many organizations see virtual training as an opportunity to save both time and money. There's no need for participants to travel or even leave their workspace to attend training. Virtual training is convenient and can be cost effective.

But is it really the right solution for your training need? This is a question that every training professional should ask before implementing a virtual training solution.

To determine if virtual training is the correct delivery method to use, consider the following questions:

1. *Are the participants centrally located or dispersed?* If your organization is not going to save on travel expenses because everyone is in the same location, then stick with face-to-face training. It may be just as fast for them to walk down the hallway to your training room as it would be for them to log in to a virtual classroom.

2. *Do all participants speak the same language?* Virtual training can be an excellent way to provide training to an international population, as long as language barriers do not get in the way.

3. *Will every participant have an appropriate learning environment?* Participants need to have their own individual computer, Internet connection, and telephone line to attend the virtual event. They should be in a quiet area conducive to learning. If they are in an open space or cubicle environment, they will need headphones or another way to tune out external noise.

4. *What technology barriers affect success?* Participants need to have the appropriate technology available to them. The exact technology needed will vary depending upon the virtual software program used; however, a typical technology setup requires a high-speed Internet connection, a sound card and speakers to hear streaming media, and administrative privileges to install software.

When virtual training is done well, it can strengthen an organization because participants from various departments and multiple locations build relationships in the classroom. They might realize that other participants are dealing with the same types of problems they are, and therefore they might be able to more easily relate to one another. Virtual training can break down regional and departmental silos when participants from various locations collaborate together. When virtual training is done well, it can lead to increased communication and, in turn, more effective business results.

Unfortunately, some trainers implement virtual training in situations that do not make sense. For instance, one organization wanted to save on telephone conference calling costs by having everyone bring their laptop to a conference meeting room so they could share a speakerphone. This setup reduces participation because it prevents appropriate breakout groups and makes it difficult to hear anyone speak. Another organization had participants attend using a computer on an open table in the frequently used employee break room. Participants reported so many external distractions that they could not stay focused on the training.

When such potentially disastrous implementations occur, it's not always the trainer's fault—sometimes it's the organization who forces the decision, and sometimes it's simply a lack of understanding about virtual training. Regardless, you should take steps to avoid these unfortunate situations.

Of course, in the face-to-face classroom, trainers frequently face implementation conditions that are not ideal. You might not have enough resources to properly execute a training plan. Or you might deal with participants who are not supported in their quest for training. In these situations, especially when things are beyond your control, manage them to the best of your ability. And it's the same in the virtual classroom. Despite our best efforts, sometimes a virtual training solution is not well supported or well designed, but the trainer needs to make the best of it and manage the situation.

Basic Rule 2

Virtual training can be an effective learning solution. However, it is not the right learning solution for every learning initiative in every organization.

See Table 1–4 for a few ideas about conducting virtual training in scenarios that are not ideal.

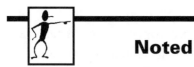

Noted

Joe Willmore's story: Discovering Virtual Training

Many years ago, I attended a conference presentation with four speakers. Two were strong organizational development (OD) professionals, and two used technology for decision making. What I took away from that presentation was that interaction in a virtual environment is not the same as it is in the face-to-face environment. Around the same time, I read some research on the dynamics of virtual teams, specifically that virtual teams build trust differently than face-to-face teams. This helped me realize early on that virtual training is not just face-to-face training with computers. It's a whole different dynamic.

—Joe Willmore, President and Founder, Willmore Consulting Group

Table 1–4. Virtual Training in Tricky Situations

Situation	Suggested Solutions
Participants in a cubicle or other less than ideal learning environments	Supply stereo telephone headsets for participants to use. Create *Do Not Disturb* signs for cubicle walls. See if participants can borrow an office or room with a closed door.
Two or more participants have to share the same computer	Plan ahead and request loaner laptops for participants. Schedule more than one virtual training session and have participants attend different classes.

Getting It Done

In your transition to delivering in the online classroom, you should be aware of the multiple definitions of virtual training. What one person considers to be virtual training may not be what someone else considers to be virtual training. Therefore, always take time to discuss training needs and intended outcomes so that everyone has a common understanding of the goal and the chosen method to get there. Once you are certain that the synchronous online classroom is part of the training solution, your next step is to learn how to transfer your training skills to this new platform.

Now that you have learned some of the basics about virtual training, use Worksheet 1–1 to help guide your journey. Then, use Worksheet 1–2 to assess your readiness.

In chapter 2, we'll review the training skills needed to be a successful virtual facilitator.

Worksheet 1–1: Goal Setting

Use the following questions to guide your journey to virtual training success.

How will learning to be an effective virtual trainer benefit you personally?

_____

How will learning to be an effective virtual trainer benefit your organization?

_____

Why is learning to be an effective virtual trainer important to you right now? What are the short-term benefits?

_____

How might learning to be an effective virtual trainer help you in the future? What are the long-term benefits?

_____

Use SMART goal setting guidelines (specific, measurable, achievable, realistic, timely) to create a learning plan for yourself.

Goal #1: _____

Goal #2: _____

Goal #3: _____

Revisit these goals frequently throughout your journey, adjusting them as necessary.

Bonus

What might get in the way of accomplishing your goals?

_____

How can you overcome these obstacles? _____

Worksheet 1–2: Preparedness Checklist

Use this worksheet to assess your readiness for virtual training. The higher your overall score, the more prepared you will be for virtual training.

1. Organizational Readiness The organization . . .	Never	Rarely	Sometimes	Usually	Always
currently uses technology for learning initiatives (i.e., self-paced e-learning for compliance training).	1	2	3	4	5
is open to trying new methods and techniques for organizational learning (i.e., early adopter of new training techniques).	1	2	3	4	5
supports learning initiatives (i.e., visible executive or key leadership support).	1	2	3	4	5

2. Technology Readiness	No	Yes
Each learner has access to a personal computer with Internet connection and all necessary software.	1	2
There are no connectivity issues for virtual classroom access (or if there are issues, they can be resolved).	1	2

3. People Readiness	No	Yes
Each learner has a private location—free of disruptions and distractions—to participate fully in virtual training.	1	2
Learners have basic computer skills (i.e., keyboard typing, basic navigation skills) and are comfortable using technology.	1	2

2

Virtual Training
Is Still Training

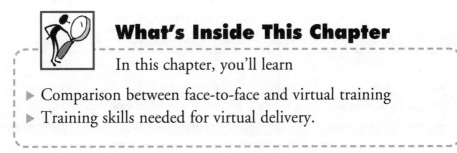

What's Inside This Chapter

In this chapter, you'll learn

▶ Comparison between face-to-face and virtual training

▶ Training skills needed for virtual delivery.

By now you may be thinking, "Oh no, I have to start all over again! Virtual training will be a career change for me because of all the new skills I need to learn!" Rest assured that if you're a classroom trainer, then you DO already know a lot about facilitating in the online classroom.

Think of it as adding a new layer to your training skill set. It's similar to learning to drive a motorcycle or bus after you already know how to drive a car. It's all transportation, so you apply your experienced driving knowledge to the new vehicle. You may need to take a class or study for an exam to drive the new transportation; however, you already know the basic skills. Likewise, many of the same face-to-face training skills are used in the virtual classroom. Yes, the environment is online and there are some significant differences, but you will not be starting from scratch.

Comparison Between Virtual and Face-to-Face Training

Many of the same training skills are used in both the face-to-face and virtual classroom. Table 2–1 provides a summary of common skills used in both delivery methods.

We will explore the nuances of these similarities later in this chapter. But first, let's focus on the differences.

There are two main differences when facilitating classes virtually:

▶ You do not see the participants.
▶ You use technology to communicate with and engage the learners.

Table 2–1. Skills Needed For Training Delivery

Training Skills	Face-to-Face Training	Virtual Training
Facilitate discussion	Yes	Yes
Ask questions	Yes	Yes
Give instructions for group activities	Yes	Yes
Teach new skills	Yes	Yes
Present content	Yes	Yes
Engage participants	Yes	Yes
Manage class time	Yes	Yes
Use technology	Sometimes	Yes
Multitask	Yes	Yes, using technology
Observe and monitor participant behavior	Yes	Yes, however trainer does not see participants' faces or body language

These differences might not seem like much on paper, but they are significant. While training skills are still used in the virtual classroom, the environment in which they are used is a whole new world.

Difference 1: No Visual Contact. You can't see the participants! For many trainers, not having visual contact is the most intimidating feature of delivering in the virtual classroom. They are disturbed by the thought of not seeing the participants. Classroom trainers are usually very good at reading participants' body language.

- They observe participants' faces to see if they are "getting it."
- They watch to see if energy levels in the room are getting low.
- They notice cues that tell them to speed up or slow down.
- They look for signals that participants are paying attention and maintaining interest in the content.

Because virtual trainers do not see participants, they have to rely on other methods of observing participants. Virtual trainers still determine if participants are getting it, and whether or not they are paying attention. They stay aware of the group's overall energy level during class.

Due to the inability to see participants in the virtual classroom, a common thought is to use video streaming. If all participants and the trainer have a webcam, and the virtual classroom software program has the capability to display video, then problem solved, right? No, unfortunately not. I do not recommend using video streaming in a synchronous virtual classroom in order to "see" the participants. Let me explain. Yes, technically you could have webcams and use the streaming video feature, but there are two drawbacks to this.

First, multiple video streams significantly increase the amount of Internet bandwidth needed for the class. The connection speed will slow down, which could negatively affect the other learning activities. If everyone's connection speed is slow, when you switch from one slide to the next, there will be lag time for the participants' screens to catch up with yours, which can be extremely distracting to the learning environment. This lag time means you may be talking about a screen that they cannot see. Therefore, weigh the potential impact these video streams will have on your class.

Second, video streaming does not usually add instructional value to the class. Instead, it can actually do more harm than help. Imagine you have 15 participants in your online class, and you asked each to turn on a webcam. On the side of the screen, you would have 16 small windows (15 plus yourself), each with a moving participant headshot. (It might remind you of the famous Brady Bunch television show opening scene, where each family member appeared in a box and traded glances with one another throughout the introductory song.) At first, this visual aid would be a fun novelty addition to the screen. You could watch them and they could watch you and each other. As class continues, however, these windows can become a distraction amidst other learning activities. They will simply do not add value to the training content.

Your next thought might be, "Well then, just have the trainers use their webcams so that participants can see them, and it's just one video stream." While it can be a good thing for participants to see the trainer, our original dilemma was the trainer not being able to watch the participants' body language during class. Showing the trainer via streaming video does not solve the problem.

Think About This

If you want the participants to see you, then show your photograph on a slide at the beginning of the session, or briefly turn on your webcam at the beginning so participants can see you, and then turn it off for the remainder of the session. Once again, the ability of the participants to see you on screen will not add much value to the training content. You can engage participants and effectively facilitate without them watching you talk.

Although I am not a fan of using a webcam during virtual training, some trainers believe it is worth the effort. Here is another viewpoint:

I've tried to experience as many different virtual sessions as possible, on a variety of subjects, with a wide variety of presenters. Since keeping people engaged is as important a goal as transferring learning, I have found that a live camera of the facilitator is critical to increasing engagement. Good facilitators can maintain eye contact and animated facial expressions that almost replicate being in the same room, from the participant's viewpoint. I found myself participating with a particularly excellent virtual facilitator, and I was nodding and smiling back as though she could see me.

—Lynne Hobbs, Training Performance Consultant, AchieveGlobal

The bottom line is that not seeing the participants is not as big of a problem as it initially seems to be. There are other ways you can "see" the participants and "watch" for the cues you need. We'll explore these techniques of how to encourage participants in chapter 8.

Difference 2: Using Technology to Communicate With and Engage Participants. In any training class, the instructor communicates with participants and leads them through a series of activities to achieve the course's stated learning objectives. The obvious difference between facilitating a face-to-face class and a virtual one is the technology used to communicate and engage. Virtual training uses special software programs specifically designed for online collaboration between multiple participants. The trainer uses these virtual tools to facilitate.

In a virtual class, the trainer can display a Microsoft Office PowerPoint slide show, write on a virtual whiteboard, invite participants to chat via instant messenger, share software applications, and more. The content of a class may be the same face to face as it is in the virtual classroom, but the delivery mechanism differs.

At first you might think that virtual training is limited to technology topics such as how to use a software application. You might also think that virtual training activities cannot match what can be done in a face-to-face class. The reality is that almost anything can be successfully taught in the virtual classroom. This includes learning new software programs, sales techniques, business acumen, interpersonal skills, or time management—anything!

Another surprising reality for some is that in the virtual classroom, you can do almost anything that a face-to-face classroom can do. Using the virtual tools both as they are intended and in creative ways, the trainer leads the class through a series of activities to achieve the course's stated learning objectives. The class can discuss, brainstorm, take notes, work in small groups, play content-related games, watch video demonstrations, and so on.

We will explore virtual classroom technology in chapter 4, and learn more about engaging participants in chapter 8. For now, let's focus specifically on the unique role of the trainer in the virtual classroom.

Noted

The biggest surprise to me was that it takes just as much energy to deliver a class virtually as it does when you have a group of people sitting in front of you. As a matter of fact, it may take even more energy for virtual delivery, because you don't have the synergy of the classroom from which to fuel yourself.

—Kathy Shurte, Manager, Training Development and
Performance Management, Florida Department of Transportation, District 4

Training Skills Used by the Virtual Trainer

The two differences noted above are significant, and they distinguish virtual training from face-to-face training. However, virtual training is still training. As listed in Table 2–1, many classroom training skills are still used. Let's review the basic training skills used by virtual and classroom trainers alike, with special focus on what's unique in the virtual classroom.

Facilitate Discussion. In both training environments—the face-to-face classroom and the virtual one—a key role of the trainer is to facilitate. Facilitation consists of

- ▶ asking questions to provoke discussion
- ▶ drawing people into conversation
- ▶ praising learners for their participation
- ▶ enabling participants to apply the learning.

Trainers ask questions for a variety of reasons. They seek responses to a query and poll the audience for input. They probe to make people think. And they ask provocative discussion questions to draw out comments. Every question a trainer asks during class should have purpose and meaning, moving the class along to the learning outcome.

The virtual environment requires the questions asked to be even more specific and directed. When asking questions during a virtual delivery, the trainer needs to not only ask the question, but also indicate how the participants should respond. For example, a trainer might ask, "Who thinks this topic is challenging?" However, in the virtual classroom, the trainer would first say, "If you think this topic is challenging, please click the 'raise hand' button," and then ask a follow-up question to a participant whose hand is raised "Sandee, tell us what you find challenging about it." This specific method of questioning lets participants know exactly what you expect of them and how they should respond to your question. In a face-to-face class, the trainer might ask, "When would you use this skill in your job?" In the virtual classroom, that same question might sound like, "Let's have everyone respond to this next question in the chat window: When would you use this skill in your job?"

Basic Rule 3

Trainers should ask very specific questions during virtual delivery, with emphasis on how participants should respond.

In addition, the trainer should also use participants' names when only one person should respond to a question (such as, "José, could you elaborate on your comment in the chat window?"). The specific direct questioning approach eliminates any confusion for participants over how to respond.

A skilled facilitator also draws each person into the discussion while maintaining a comfortable classroom environment. (A comfortable environment means they don't embarrass people or put them on the spot in a painful way.) A successful trainer strives to create and maintain a comfortable environment because it helps participants more easily learn. So in the virtual classroom, to draw people into the discussion, the trainer might ask for a response "from someone we haven't heard from yet." Learners can also be drawn into the discussion when trainers use their names, or by referring back to something a participant said earlier in the class.

One way to keep the facilitation evenly distributed is to keep track of who is contributing to the class discussion. I do this by printing out a roster prior to the session, and making tick marks next to participant names when they share examples. If participants stay quiet, then I'll find an opportunity to ask them direct questions and encourage their contributions.

Think About This

When asking a direct question to a participant, ensure it is a question that has no wrong answer. In other words, when you call on someone by name, make it a question that could have any response. For example, "Bryan, what is the square root of 362?" would not be appropriate because it has one specific right answer. However, "Bryan, what did you think about the video demonstration?" would be fine. This helps maintain a comfortable learning environment.

Great facilitation techniques also include providing positive feedback for participation. Thank your attendees for completing an exercise. Use positive reinforcement phrases ("good" or "excellent") when someone answers a question. Use names to encourage specific individuals. Praise learners frequently for their engagement when they contribute to the discussion. Also praise them when they use the virtual classroom tools. These reinforcement techniques should be used in any training environment, including the virtual one.

A word about virtual class size: In order for the trainer to effectively facilitate discussion, the class size should be conducive to participation. Class size is as important in the virtual classroom as it is in the face-to-face one. While there is no standard rule for the number of people to have in a virtual class, the number should be large enough to successfully complete the group learning activities and small enough so that everyone can contribute to a discussion. My preference is to have no more than 16 participants so that each person can receive my individual attention during class.

Finally, great facilitators create opportunities for participants to apply the learning. This fact is true regardless of the delivery method—face-to-face or virtual. Therefore, as a virtual trainer, encourage participants to share their own stories. Allow time for them to hear their fellow participants' experiences. Help participants see how the training topic can be immediately applied and how it's relevant to them. Give opportunity to experiment and practice. These methods will lead to a beneficial program for the participants geared toward the learning objectives.

Give Instructions for Group Activities. One of the trainer's primary responsibilities is to lead participants from one activity to the next during class. Give clear directions for each exercise and set expectations with the participants.

If activity directions are not clear, confusion and frustration result. Participants are more likely to disengage from the class if they do not have a complete grasp on what they are supposed to be doing at any given time.

When you give activity instructions, there are two guidelines that are true in both training environments but warrant special attention in the virtual classroom.

- ▶ *Be explicitly clear about every intricate detail of the exercise.* Participants need to know exactly what buttons to click, where to type their responses, what to watch for, or what is expected of them during the allotted time.
- ▶ *Give directions both verbally and visually.* Participants need to both see and hear the instructions for comprehension and retention. Providing directions verbally helps participants understand what to do. Providing directions visually helps those who process information by sight. A visual aid with instructions also allows participants to refer back to them during the exercise. This visual aid can either be on screen or in a participant handout that is printed prior to class.

Manage Class Time. As a trainer, have you ever been rushed to finish a class? Or realized too late that you have more information than time? Or wondered why some of your training classes finish early and others leave you gasping for air? Even the most seasoned trainers sometimes struggle with classroom time management.

Time management concerns are amplified in the virtual classroom because synchronous online classes are often shorter in length. Every single minute counts. Think about it: If you have an eight-hour, face-to-face class and you lose five minutes due to a discussion tangent, you can easily make it up at another point during the day. But in a 60-minute virtual session, if you spend an extra unplanned five minutes on a topic, then you've lost almost 10 percent of your available time!

Maximize every minute of your classroom time. Good time management will help you have credibility with your audience and make the most of your time together. For example, if you have a face-to-face class scheduled to begin at 9 a.m., and you start a few minutes late because you were sipping on water while walking to the front of the room, the participants would not think much of it because they can visually see you and know that it is time to start class. However, in the virtual environment, if you start a few minutes late for any reason, your participants may think, "Did I get the wrong time?" and they might disconnect from the session. Also, you may have to scramble to make up that time during the class.

Think About This

It's a best practice for virtual training classes to be 60–90 minutes, and no more than 120 minutes in length. If your sessions have to be longer, build in time for a break.

When you prepare for your virtual session, make sure you clearly know how much time each activity should take and how much discussion time you have. It's up to you to manage the pace of class.

Review Table 2–2, which will help you recognize and eliminate the most common time wasters in the virtual classroom.

Table 2–2. Dealing With Time Wasters

Time Waster	Suggested Solution
Taking too much time on introductions	Use a brief activity, such as a poll, to learn about your audience instead of asking them to introduce themselves one by one.
Wasting time reviewing logistics	Share logistics prior to the class start time, either via email or on an introductory screen.
Spending too much time showing how to use the virtual classroom software tools	Require a prerequisite session on how to use the virtual classroom software. Invite new users to join the session early for review.
Requiring an answer (or response) from each participant	Use one of the software tools—poll, shared whiteboard, or chat—to allow for simultaneous responses.
Not seeking input from participants on the timing and pacing of activities	Ask participants to electronically "raise their hands" when finished with an exercise so you know when it's time to move on.

Establish Ground Rules. The ground rules of a training class let participants know what behaviors are expected and which ones are not allowed. Typical ground rules for any type of class might include

- follow common courtesies for communication
- keep sensitive information confidential
- be on time
- share experiences
- participate actively.

Trainers should always establish ground rules in a training class, regardless of the delivery environment. Ground rules unique to a virtual class may include

- state your name before speaking
- never use your telephone "hold" button
- use mute/unmute buttons if in a noisy environment
- ask questions verbally or via the chat window at any time.

I believe it is important for participants to set their own ground rules. In my face-to-face classes, I may start the list with suggestions, but then ask the group to decide upon the rules. Once the rules are established, I'll often joke with the group, using an analogy from the airlines, by saying, "When someone sits in an exit row, they have to verbally agree to follow the airline's rules for emergency exit seating. Here in our class, we also need to verbally agree to follow these rules." Giving participants input to the ground rules list increases the likelihood of them being kept. I also ask participants to decide the "penalty" for breaking a rule. My face-to-face classes have come up with some fun and creative ideas, such as asking the offender to wear a funny straw hat for five minutes. What works for one group may not work for another, which is why the participants have control.

In a virtual class, ground rules should still be established, and the participants should still have ownership of them. They can decide their own penalties for the rule breakers, such as asking the offender to sing a short song. The two main differences in a virtual class are the amount of time available for ground rules discussion and the types of ground rules to include.

Since virtual classes are often shorter in length than their face-to-face counterparts, you should limit the amount of time spent on logistics. Group together virtual class "housekeeping" items and the ground rules into one short discussion. You could even cover these prior to the class start time by having this information posted on screen while you're waiting for class to begin. If you use this technique, then gain the participants' buy-in to the rules with a quick question at the beginning of class.

If you have a group of participants new to virtual training, then you may need to take a more active role in establishing ground rules. You can give them a list and ask which ones they agree with and what else they would add.

Getting It Done

Virtual training is still training. You will be able to transfer many of your classroom training skills to the virtual environment. Yes, the online dynamic is different. Yes, you will use technology to communicate. No, you cannot see the participants. However, despite these obstacles, you are not starting over from square one when you transition from the face-to-face classroom to the virtual classroom. It will take time and practice to get comfortable with the new delivery method; however, you can successfully make the leap. Reading this book is a good step in the right direction. Use Worksheet 2–1 to assess your skills in delivering training to the virtual classroom.

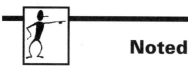

Noted

Kella Price, CEO, Human Resources and Training Consultant—Price Consulting Group, has advice for classroom trainers who are just getting started with virtual delivery: Think about all the things you like when you are participating in a training . . . incorporate those elements into your own delivery. Ask others to critique your course before using it with participants. Try to use some the activities that you would do in a traditional classroom in the online environment . . . group activities and breakouts are possible in many virtual platforms.

Worksheet 2–1: Training Skills Assessment

Place a checkmark next to the training skills you would like to focus on learning to deliver in the virtual classroom.

Facilitate discussion	
Ask questions	
Give instructions for group activities	
Teach new skills	
Present content	
Engage participants	
Manage class time	
Use technology	
Multitask	
Monitor participant behavior	

What skill(s) are already your areas of strength?

_____

What skill(s) will you focus on first in preparing to deliver in the virtual classroom?

_____

3

Learn About Technology

- -

 What's Inside This Chapter

In this chapter, you'll learn

▶ The basics of hardware and software
▶ Files and folder structure
▶ Internet features specific to virtual training
▶ Types of telephony in virtual training
▶ The importance of learning more about technology.

To be a successful virtual trainer, you must learn about technology. You need to know more than the virtual classroom software—you also need to know what's underneath it.

It's similar to driving a car. You can be a good driver without knowing how to change a tire or check the oil. But when a problem arises, you are dependent on someone else to fix it. You may be waiting on the side of the road while everyone else passes you by.

Classroom trainers are faced with the same reality. The best classroom trainers are ones who not only facilitate with ease, but they have mastered all aspects of the classroom including its technology. They can connect a laptop to any projector, show videos on any DVD player, and use standard sound systems. They can perform basic troubleshooting when things go wrong. They are not dependent on someone else for these essential classroom functions.

The more you know about technology, the more comfortable you'll be in the virtual classroom. You'll be able to troubleshoot when things go wrong, it will be easier for you to multitask, and your classes will flow more smoothly. You'll also be seen with greater credibility by your participants.

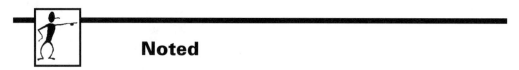

Noted

I understand how important technology is to the way we do business today, and I want to learn it.

—Kathy Shurte, CPLP, Manager, Training Development and
Performance Management, Florida Department of Transportation, District 4

The Basics of Hardware and Software

For those of you who already know basic technology, bear with me while we make sure everyone is on the same page. Or, skip ahead to the Tech Check at the end of this section.

Let's start with the basics: hardware and software.

Hardware consists of the physical components you can touch. Your desktop computer, monitor, mouse, printer, cables, keyboard, hard drives, and removable drives are all considered hardware. Your laptop, PDA, or smartphone would also be considered hardware.

The computer's processor is the brain and central nervous system of the computer—accepting commands and telling the various parts what to do and how to respond. Some of these hardware items take input (mouse, keyboard, touch screen), while others give output (monitor or screen, printer).

To participate in virtual training, and to facilitate an online class, you'll need a basic computer setup: computer, monitor, mouse, and keyboard, plus a sound card and speakers if you plan to use any sound-enabled features in class. Most laptops have all of these hardware components built-in.

Basic Rule 4

It's possible to use Internet-enabled smartphones to participate in some virtual training classes. However, given their current size and software limitations, it is not recommended that you use one to facilitate.

Software, on the other hand, are the intangible programs that tell the computer processor how to function and what to do. Software falls into two categories: operating systems and traditional applications. Examples of operating systems are Microsoft Windows, Linux, and Mac OS X (*pronounced Oh-Ess-Ten*) Snow Leopard. Examples of what I call traditional applications are Microsoft Office Excel, Word, and PowerPoint.

Think About This

If you want to play your favorite song, you need both hardware and software. The hardware would be a CD player and its speakers, or it could be your iPod and headphones. When you press the buttons to find the song you wish to hear, and adjust sound controls such as bass, treble, and volume, you're using software to do those tasks. The result? Hearing beautiful music.

Every software program has its specialty. If I visited your town and asked where the best steak restaurant was, you'd send me to the place known for great steak. And you'd expect me to order a steak when I got there. Would I go and order spaghetti? No. It's possible to order spaghetti, some people probably do, but the point of going to the best steakhouse in town is to enjoy what its known for: the steak. It's the same with software programs—they each have their specialties. They may have a menu full of choices, and a kitchen capable of cooking a variety of cuisine, but each restaurant—and each software program—has a sweet spot, or what it does best.

The virtual classroom uses a special type of software program that allows multiple computers to see the same screen at the same time and to collaborate together. We'll explore the details of these types of classroom software programs in chapter 4.

Other software programs that virtual trainers commonly use include Microsoft Office PowerPoint, Adobe Acrobat Reader (PDF), and Internet browsers such as Microsoft Internet Explorer or Apple Safari.

Speaking of the Internet, Internet software can be an entire category unto itself. We use software programs to access the Internet such as Microsoft Internet Explorer, Mozilla Firefox, Apple Safari, or Google Chrome. We also use software programs, such as Adobe Flash Player to view certain Internet content. And Internet software can help us use other Internet software, such as the case with Google Toolbar, which helps speed web searches and adds other browser functionality.

Traditional software is usually installed on your computer from a storage location such as a CD-ROM, USB drive, or your organization's network servers. Internet software is usually downloaded onto your computer by visiting a vendor's website.

In order for hardware and software to talk to one another, they need "drivers." You may have experienced working with drivers if you've ever installed a printer. You need the correct driver on your computer in order to be able to print to that printer. Some Internet software, including certain virtual classroom and collaboration programs, also need to have drivers installed. In my experience, drivers are not a frequent cause of problems during a virtual training class, but they are something to keep in the back of your mind when troubleshooting incorrect display or other settings. We'll explore troubleshooting in chapter 10.

Software Plug-Ins and Administrator Rights. Some software programs make use of "plug-ins" (also called "add-ins") to enhance their capabilities. Plug-ins are like little software programs that stay hidden in the background until they are needed. Plug-ins have various functions, such as playing video or audio clips. For example, when you play a video in a virtual classroom software program, it could use a plug-in like Apple QuickTime or Adobe Flash Player.

Like traditional software programs, add-ins are installed or downloaded onto a computer. Some virtual classroom software requires plug-ins to work properly. This is where problems may arise, because computers can be programmed to allow only certain users the ability to install software or make changes to their computer settings. If a participant does not have administrator rights to his or her computer, then the computer may not be able to install required add-ins for the virtual classroom software programs.

Trainers should check with the Information Technology (IT) or Information Services (IS) department of their organization to see if there will be any known challenges with installing necessary plug-ins or administrative rights assigned to participants' computers.

Basic Rule 5

To check a computer to see if it will be able to use your virtual classroom software program, click on the "test" link provided by the software vendor. This link is usually included in the automated event registration email, or available on the vendor's website.

Settings. Most hardware and software programs have settings that can be changed by a user with administrative privileges. Some settings are based on the type of hardware you have, while other settings are changed because of user preference.

For example, your monitor has various display settings. Some monitors display a screen resolution that is 1024 pixels wide by 768 pixels high. Other common resolutions are 800 × 600 or 1280 × 800. The screen resolution dictates the output quality and size display seen on a monitor.

When delivering virtual training, your computer's screen resolution settings might be different than the settings on your participants' computers. Therefore, what you see on your computer screen may not exactly be the same image as what your participants see on their computer screens. Everyone's screens will look similar, yet there may be distortions or other slight differences.

It may be helpful to think of it this way: When you play a music CD on different systems, you hear the same song but with slightly different experiences. The sound quality depends on the speakers, as well as the player's sound settings such as bass, treble, and balance. The result is a slightly different listening experience based on the hardware and software used.

Therefore, as a virtual trainer you should have a general understanding of what settings can be changed on a computer and know how to change the basic settings of your own computer.

By now you're probably thinking: Do I really need to know these technology details? Let's just get to the good stuff—how to deliver training in the virtual classroom. The answer is yes—you really do need to know these technology details.

Think about a classroom trainer who uses a projector to display a visual. If the projected display is crooked or slightly out of focus, then everyone in the class notices. They focus on the imperfections, and wonder why the trainer doesn't fix it. On the other hand, if a classroom trainer uses a projector and the visual display is perfect, then no one pays attention to the mechanics. Instead, they're focused on learning.

Classroom trainers who know how to adjust projectors, including all of the menu commands such as keystone and other display settings, are able to keep participants' focus off the technology and on the class.

It's really the same in the virtual classroom. Once you've mastered the technology, including this behind-the-scenes look at it, you and your participants will simply use these tools and everyone can focus on the learning.

Files and Folders

Another important technology component are files and the folder structure where you store them. There are two main reasons a virtual trainer needs to know about files and folders. First, you need to know what file types work (and don't work) with your virtual classroom software. Second, you need to know where your files are stored and how to get to them quickly when needed.

File Types. Every software program saves its files with a unique signature called a file type. The file type is readily apparent by either looking at the file extension (if it's visible), or by looking at the icon graphic next to the file name. These file extensions associate the file with a particular software program.

When you are delivering in the virtual classroom, you use files to communicate visually. For example, a Microsoft Office PowerPoint presentation file shows slides with text and graphics or a media file could play a video to demonstrate a new skill. You might also have a poll question saved or a document you wish to refer to during class. All of these files are opened or "shared" in your virtual classroom.

When software programs are updated to newer versions, sometimes the file extensions change as well. For example, previous versions of Microsoft Office PowerPoint files had a .ppt extension, yet the default setting for PowerPoint 2007 files is .pptx.

It's important to know what file types are supported by your virtual classroom software. Every program is different, so you should know what works for your chosen software.

File Storage. Trainers use files in both the face-to-face classroom and the virtual classroom. A face-to-face classroom trainer has instructor notes, participant hand-outs, flipcharts, and videos. In the virtual classroom, a trainer uses all of the above and more. Virtual training files could also include poll questions, saved chat notes, and other shared documents.

Your electronic files are stored in drives and folders, similar to how you store paper files in your office filing cabinet. Your file organization structure is not critically important: You may be an extremely organized "filer" and have every file in its place, with hanging folders and color-coded labels. Or, you may be a "piler," with everything thrown into piles. Your computer filing cabinet is probably the same: files organized in subfolders or collected in one big folder. What *is* important is being able to find the training file you need at a moment's notice. Therefore, it really doesn't matter what your style is, as long as you can find the file you need when you need it.

In the virtual classroom, in order to share a document or to open a saved poll question, you must know the name of the file, where you saved it, and how to navigate to that location. You need to be able to get to it quickly. You should also know how to make back-up copies of your files, and how to email file attachments to participants. These things are essential skills for a virtual trainer.

The Internet

Virtual classroom software, by its very nature, uses the Internet. Therefore, virtual trainers should know basic Internet features.

Connection Types. A fairly important consideration is the type of Internet connection that you and your participants have. The connection needs to be fast enough to handle the virtual classroom software and all of the activities you have planned. If you plan to use any streaming video during the class, you'll want to ensure everyone's Internet speeds are fast enough to handle it.

While most corporate Internet connections are fast, consider the home office user or someone using a public wireless hotspot. Those connections are more likely to be slower or not as robust.

Firewalls and Pop-Up Blockers. Due to security concerns on the Internet, most computers today have software to prevent unauthorized intrusions. While this is normally a good thing, it can get in the way of virtual classroom software programs.

A firewall is a virtual barrier that, for security reasons, separates a computer or network from others. It not only prevents unauthorized entry to the network, it can also prevent outbound connections. Firewalls typically do not get in the way on personal home computers. But an organization's firewall for its corporate computers might interfere with a virtual software program. Therefore, it's important for a trainer to check with the IT or IS department of the organization ahead of time to see if there will be any known challenges with firewalls or other security features.

Another security element found on most Internet-connected computers are pop-up blockers. These blockers prevent "pop-up" windows from opening in a computer's Internet browser. Once again, this is usually a good thing, but it can also get in the way of some virtual classroom software programs that open in a new pop-up window.

Pop-up blockers can usually be disabled by the computer's user, although sometimes multiple pop-up blockers can be installed and in use at one time. My favorite trick is to press the CTRL key on the keyboard while clicking on a link, because that manually overrides any pop-up blockers.

Cookies and Caches. As you log in to some websites, a small file is deposited into your computer with identifying information such as your computer's IP address or which pages you view while on the site. These small files are referred to as cookies. Some virtual classroom software programs need to have an Internet browser's cookies enabled in order to capture log in information. You should know if your computer has security settings that prevent cookies from being deposited.

These cookies are stored in a tucked-away location called a cache, along with other temporary Internet files. When an Internet browser is having display problems or log in problems, a common troubleshooting technique is to clear out the browser's cache and to clear out its cookies.

Virtual trainers should know how to clear the Internet cache and delete unwanted cookies. In most Internet browser programs, including Microsoft Internet Explorer, Firefox Mozilla, and Google Chrome, this option can be found in dialogue boxes under the Tools menu.

Telephony

During a virtual training class, you'll have three types of connections: visual, kinesthetic, and auditory. The visual connection is what's seen on the screen. Kinesthetic is the physical movement associated with the connection, such as typing on the keyboard. And the audio connection is hearing everyone's dialogue.

Your computer handles the visual and kinesthetic connections to the virtual training class, and your telephone usually handles the audio. *Telephony* is a broad term referring to overall audio connection and telephone equipment used.

There are three types of audio connections you and the participants could use:

1. Standalone conference call
2. Integrated conference call
3. Voice over Internet Protocol (VoIP).

With a stand-alone conference call, everyone dials a pre-established telephone number. This conference call is not connected in any way to the virtual classroom software. Sometimes these numbers are referred to as a "conference bridge" and are often managed by a telephony vendor.

Integrated conference calling connects both the virtual classroom software and the conference bridge. One vendor supplies both the software and telephony, and the moderator of one is the moderator of the other. With integrated conference calling, everyone still uses his or her telephone to dial into the audio portion of the call. One advantage of an integrated telephony connection is that some virtual classroom software programs display the participants' telephone connection status, and the trainer is able to view and change individual settings (such as placing a participant on mute).

Also, an integrated conference call often includes the ability for participants to dial-in or to receive a phone call from the conference service. My personal preference is for participants to dial-in, so that they can decide what time to pick up the phone and dial.

The third type of conference calling used for virtual classes is Voice over Internet Protocol, or VoIP for short. (VoIP can either be pronounced as one syllable "voyp" or spelled out "vee-oh-eye-pee.")

VoIP uses the Internet and computer's microphone and speakers to transmit the audio portion of the call. Instead of using a telephone for the conference call, participants simply connect to the conference and speak into their computer's microphone. They hear the trainer and other participants through their computer's speakers.

People frequently ask if they can use a cell phone to participate in or facilitate virtual training. The answer is yes, provided there is a clear connection signal without static or the chance of a dropped call. A telephone is a telephone, regardless of the type of connection it has. VoIP telephones can be used as well. The bottom line is that the first two audio methods listed above require some type of telephone connection. The third type, VoIP, simply uses the computer, its hardware components, and its Internet connection.

For example, my home office telephone uses VoIP for its connection. I do not have traditional telephone service to my house; instead, my phone service travels over my Internet connection. So, when I deliver a virtual training class that uses the first two options, I use my laptop to log in to the virtual classroom software and use my telephone to dial the conference call number. While they both use the Internet, they are separate connections to the virtual class.

Virtual trainers should know common commands used by the conference call provider, such as how to mute and unmute lines, and whether or not the audio conference supports audio subgroups or "breakout rooms."

Learn More About Technology

I've always felt fortunate that my training career began as a software trainer when personal computers first became mainstream in office environments. I learned and taught DOS programming, the first version of Microsoft Windows, early versions of today's common office programs, and basic networking. This experience allowed me to become very comfortable with technology.

Since I was teaching others how to use technology, I wanted to know as much as I could about it, and why it acted the way it did. So I read every software manual from cover to cover (this was when software programs came with printed instruction manuals). I clicked on every button, experimented with every feature, and learned as many shortcuts and tips as I could find.

This has remained my approach to learning new technology: reading the documentation, trying it out, and playing around with it. It's also what I recommend for trainers who are just learning a new piece of technology.

Perhaps you are like most trainers I encounter: You are self-taught in technology. You know how to get online, read email, type a letter, and fumble through a spreadsheet. You learn new technology when you have to, either by trial and error or when someone shows you a new trick. This method is common, and it works for most people. However, now that you are training in the virtual classroom, you should learn as much as you can about technology. It will serve to your advantage.

One Trainer's Journey: Learning About Technology

Kathy Shurte's Story

I am truly "the accidental" virtual trainer. Technology is not my forte, so I did not seek out opportunities to play (or frustrate myself) with the latest toys. The organizations I worked for tended to be very restrictive with technology, so I wasn't learning virtual skills at work. However, I totally understand how important technology is to the way we do business today, and I do want to learn.

Through a volunteer position with ASTD, I gained experience working on virtual teams. We did most of our work via teleconference and, as time went on, there were opportunities to participate in webinars as both a participant and a presenter. It was a great confidence builder! We also had a "tech" team at our service, and I called on them when needed.

Although I was not an early adopter, when I was ready to stick my toe in the water, I did it surrounded by a strong support network. For my training sessions, I selected topics about which I was passionate, and that made it easy for me to focus on the message and not get caught up in the medium. I also reached out to the most tech savvy people I knew and asked them for advice. Curiously, most of them were not trainers; they were just very technically astute people. And more curiously, they were telling me to do things that, as a trainer, I knew I should do: Engage your learners. Don't read from your slides. Ask questions, lots of questions. Pretty soon, my self-talk was saying, "See, you already know how to do this!" The learning, for me, was all about the technology.

Basic Rule 6

If there's one traditional software program that a virtual trainer should know well, it's Microsoft Office PowerPoint.

Most virtual classroom software programs expect the trainer to share or upload a PowerPoint file and, therefore, it becomes the foundational basis for the training. PowerPoint slides can display text, graphics, charts, and can help organize the class materials.

Trainers should know at a minimum the following features of PowerPoint:

- Inserting new slides
- Adding text, clipart, and other graphics (such as photos)
- Formatting text and graphics
- Changing slide order and deleting slides
- Adding slide animations
- Working with slide masters.

Getting It Done

Remember, technology is simply a means to an end. It's not our goal. Instead, it helps us reach our goal. We want to know it so we can use it. We want to master it so that we can manage it. Use Worksheet 3–1 to assess what types of technology you want to learn more about.

In order to be a successful virtual trainer, you must become comfortable with technology—not for the sake of technology, but for the sake of your training. In chapter 4, we'll cover the typical capabilities of virtual classroom software and how to present online.

Worksheet 3–1: Tech Check

Place a checkmark next to the technology skills you want to learn more about:

	Technology Item
_____	Computer hardware and software
_____	Internet
_____	Software programs, such as Microsoft Office PowerPoint
_____	Telephony

How will you learn about each one? List the resources you will use. (See the References in the back of this book for some ideas.)

- _____
- _____
- _____
- _____
- _____

Master Virtual Classroom Software Programs

What's Inside This Chapter

In this chapter, you'll learn

▶ How to select a virtual solution
▶ How to compare virtual classroom software programs
▶ Virtual class logistics
▶ Common features of virtual classroom software programs.

Master craftsmen know their tools: carpenters know their hammers and saws, masons know their bricks and mortar, potters know their clay, and trainers should know their virtual classroom software.

Becoming a master of your trade means being an expert in the tools you use—which means virtual trainers simply must learn everything there is to know about the software platform on which they stand. Just like a regular classroom trainer studies presentation skills and flipchart drawing techniques, a virtual trainer should study the software program they will use when delivering.

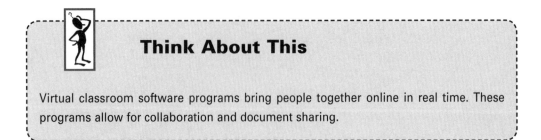

Think About This

Virtual classroom software programs bring people together online in real time. These programs allow for collaboration and document sharing.

Selecting a Virtual Solution

Selecting virtual classroom software to use can be a daunting task. It's a big decision to make: Which software platform will you use for training? The features and functions available to you in the virtual classroom depend largely on the software chosen; therefore, it's not a decision to make lightly. For example, if you know that using small-group breakout rooms will be an essential component of your online training, then you want to look for a program that has breakout rooms.

In many organizations, the information technology (IT) department has control over which software programs everyone will use. If that's the case, you should establish a good relationship with the IT decision makers and discuss your training requirements with them. When the IT department purchases a solution, you want it to be one that fits the organization's training needs.

Online virtual collaboration tools often have more than one version with different features for each, and someone outside the training function might not think about what is necessary for a virtual class. For instance, one popular virtual platform, Cisco WebEx, has three versions: Meeting Center, Training Center, and Event Center. While each has a similar look and feel, each one has its own features and capabilities. This is similar to physical meeting space. Think about where different types of training events are held in your office: conference rooms, training classrooms, and auditoriums. Virtual meeting programs have similar types of options.

Basic Rule 7

If you are scheduled to facilitate an online training class, and they tell you which virtual software platform you'll be using, be sure to ask, "Which version?"

So often I hear trainers say, "Our IT department purchased the 'meeting' version of the virtual software, and I'm trying to convince them to upgrade to the 'training' version." Nip this problem in the bud by working together with the IT team to make a purchasing decision that's right for everyone.

Comparing Virtual Classroom Software Programs

There are many competing software programs on the market today that are used for virtual classrooms. These programs are called by various names; some are referred to as online collaboration platforms, others are known as synchronous learning systems, and still others are called web conferencing programs. Since this book focuses on virtual training, I'll refer to them as virtual classroom software programs.

Table 4–1 lists a few of the most common programs currently in use by virtual trainers. Please note that this is not an exhaustive list, and it may not include the right solution for your organization. You should research thoroughly your own delivery needs, compare vendors and solutions, talk with your IT department about resource requirements, and make an informed decision. Most of these programs have trial versions for testing and allow you to participate in online sessions to familiarize yourself with the available features.

In addition to the software program vendors, several third-party vendors re-sell virtual classroom software solutions. These vendors provide additional support services for the programs, such as event management and customer support. They also package together conference calling systems and web conferencing (virtual classroom software) into one bundled solution for subscription purchase by individuals and organizations. When you use these bundled packages, the web and audio conferencing are integrated together.

Some third-party vendors call the software programs by another name. For example, Premiere Global Services, Inc. (www.pgi.com) offers a web conferencing solution called "ReadyCast," which uses Cisco WebEx software in addition to its other services. So, a trainer who delivers a virtual class using ReadyCast would need to learn how to use WebEx.

Another third-party vendor, InterCall (www.intercall.com), also offers web conferencing solutions along with its other professional services. Some of its current services include Cisco WebEx, Microsoft Office Live Meeting, and Adobe Acrobat Connect Pro. Once again, virtual trainers using these InterCall solutions should learn the underlying platforms.

Table 4–1. Selected Virtual Classroom Software Programs

Name	Website	Notes
Adobe Acrobat Connect Pro	www.adobe.com	A web conferencing program based on the Adobe Flash Player software that can be used for virtual training delivery. It integrates with other Adobe products including Adobe Presenter and Adobe Captivate.
Cisco WebEx	www.webex.com	Three versions that can be used for virtual training: Meeting Center, Training Center, and Event Center. Training Center is the preferred version for a virtual training class; however, the other versions also can be used.
Citrix GoToWebinar	www.gotowebinar.com	Online event products, including GoToMeeting and GoToWebinar. GoToWebinar is the preferred version for a virtual training class; however, other versions can also be used.
Elluminate Live!	www.elluminate.com	A virtual environment for learning. It integrates with other Elluminate products such as Elluminate Plan! and Elluminate Publish!
Microsoft Live Meeting	www.microsoft.com/ livemeeting	Online meeting space that can be used as a virtual classroom and integrates with other Microsoft products, including Microsoft Office Outlook.

The decision to use a third-party vendor versus going straight to the software vendor will depend upon your organization's overall web conferencing needs. On the one hand, if you need both audio and web conferencing, the third-party vendors provide integrated solutions. On the other hand, you may not need all of the services offered through these bundles. It's important for you to research thoroughly and decide appropriately.

Noted

Spend time practicing leading the content and working with the technology.
—Rebecca Ward, Training Performance Consultant, AchieveGlobal

Tips for Learning a Virtual Classroom Software Program.

▶ Read the Help screens in the software program.
▶ Go through the online tutorials available on the vendor website.
▶ Participate in user group discussion boards.
▶ Attend sessions that use the software program as a participant (note: most vendors offer free virtual sessions).
▶ Practice delivering sessions using the program. Set up multiple "mock" computers, or ask your friends, family, or co-workers to join as participants.
▶ Log in to a practice virtual event as a participant and click on every button and menu item to find out what each one does. Then do the same thing while logged in to the practice virtual event as the host and/or presenter. This way you will experience every button and every command from all perspectives.

Think About This

Put some thought into the type of virtual classroom program you will use, and choose the best platform for your unique needs. For a more in-depth comparison of the programs, check out the following resources:

• eLearning Guild's 360° Research Report "Synchronous Learning Systems," available at www.elearningguild.com

• Training Media Review's "Web conferencing application reviews and ratings," available at www.tmreview.com

Virtual Class Logistics

In order for a synchronous online training class to happen, the event needs to be scheduled using the software program's administration tools. This administrative task establishes parameters such as

- class date and time
- duration of the class
- presenter, trainer, or host log in details
- participant log in details
- audio or conference call features.

In addition, depending upon what virtual classroom software you are using, the administrative setup may also determine

- whether or not a participant password will be required to log in
- how early the participants can enter the event
- what entry or lobby screens the participant sees upon log in
- what privileges the participant will have in the session.

Basic Rule 8

The virtual class event setup can dictate which features will be available and who can attend. Be sure you are familiar with your virtual classroom software's administrative tools.

Most virtual classroom software programs are time-driven with a specific date and time for the event. However, for some programs, the administrative setup "generates" the meeting room, which can then be perpetually used from that point forward. For example, when using Adobe Acrobat Connect Pro, the administrator creates an online meeting room, and it can be accessed at any time. This is a useful feature because trainers can set up the room well in advance of the session. In the time-driven event programs, the trainer simply logs in early to set up the session before its start time.

The specific directions on how to schedule the event will vary from vendor to vendor and from program to program. Regardless of who is responsible in your organization for learning administration, you should learn how your software program's administration features work so that you can step in if needed. You'll also have an understanding of what can and cannot be changed for the event.

Part of event administration also includes communicating details to participants. The communication should include

- prerequisites for the course
- assignments to complete prior to the session
- handouts to print prior to the session
- technical or computer system requirements
- computer technology checks that should be completed prior to the session
- connection details for the event.

We'll review more details about communicating with participants in chapter 5.

Think About This

Most virtual classroom software programs have one log in passcode for the trainer and a separate one for the participants. (Depending on the software program, the trainer code may be called the host code, the presenter code, or the moderator code.) The trainer's passcode gives the trainer additional permissions and privileges in the software. Therefore, the trainer code should not be shared with participants. However, the trainer should know both codes for the event just in case a participant needs help logging in.

A virtual class has more technical logistics than a face-to-face one, and special care should be taken to ensure all of the details are established and communicated to everyone involved.

A small glitch in the setup of a physical class might not be a big deal, but it could spell disaster for a virtual event. For example, a training class scheduled to be held in Room 107B may be accidentally communicated to participants as Room 107A; when the participants show up to the wrong room, they could easily be redirected to the correct location. And most participants would not think twice about having to walk a few extra steps to get to the right room. However, if virtual class participants are sent the wrong event link to join the online session, we may not have an easy way to communicate the correct connection information to them in a timely manner. And participants who cannot connect to the virtual classroom may quickly give up and abandon joining the class. The incorrect link could have been a simple administrative error, yet it could be perceived as a technical glitch in the system. If this happened, your participants could miss the session, and for those who do arrive, it would be a rocky start to the virtual class.

Think About This

Take caution with your trainer passcodes. I learned this lesson the hard way when someone logged in to my training session as the host while I was in the middle of the class. It immediately bumped me out of the host role and into a participant role. I lost technical control of the class. I had to send the person a chat message requesting that they log out or at least change my role back to the host. Fortunately, she did so quickly, and I regained technical control of the class.

Later, we found out that two classes had been scheduled at the same time, and another trainer had accidentally received my event host information for her class. She quickly realized the error, logged out, and found her correct class information.

Virtual Classroom Software Roles. Speaking of learning administration, a successful virtual training event needs someone to organize all of its logistics. This person may or may not be the trainer. Just like a face-to-face classroom event, a learning coordinator might be assigned to manage the session details or the trainer could do it all.

There are the four roles required for a successful virtual class:

▶ administrator (sometimes called coordinator)
▶ host (sometimes called producer)

- ▶ trainer (sometimes called presenter)
- ▶ participants (sometimes called attendees).

Review Table 4–2 for a description of each of these roles.

There is often overlap between these roles. One person may wear multiple hats. It's possible for one trainer to act as administrator, host, and presenter. Or, there might be separate individuals available to take on each role.

It is a best practice to have at least two people involved in the administration during a live synchronous event: one person to act as host/producer and another person to act as trainer/presenter. The larger the class size, the more important it is to have multiple people responsible for the event. This shared arrangement allows the trainer to focus on the facilitation, learning, and participant engagement, while the producer focuses on the technical details. For example, if a virtual class has 12 participants, and one of them has a technical challenge, the producer can assist that person while the trainer facilitates discussion with the other 11. The producer and

Table 4–2. Roles in the Virtual Classroom

Role	Description
Administrator (sometimes called coordinator)	• Establishes online event details prior to the event • Communicates logistics to the trainer and participants
Host (sometimes called producer)	• Greets participants upon entering the classroom • Manages the technical details of the event, such as monitoring the chat window for questions, creating breakout groups, and loading polls • Troubleshoots technical problems during the event
Trainer (sometimes called presenter)	• Facilitates learning • Teaches new skills • Engages participants through discussion and activities
Participants (sometimes called attendees)	• Attends the event to learn new skills

trainer should coordinate ahead of time to explicitly determine who will do what and how the handoffs between them will occur.

Common Features of a Virtual Classroom Software Program

Let's review the common features available in most virtual classroom software programs. We'll briefly discuss each tool, its common uses for virtual training, and any unique characteristics to be mindful of when using it.

Once again, this is not an exhaustive list of all features—just the ones regularly used in virtual training. You should double check with your software program to discover which features it has, what is unique about the tool in that program, and if any software updates have changed its functionality since this book was written.

Sharing Documents. *Description:* Sharing documents is one of the most commonly used features in a virtual class. The trainer uploads a file into a viewing window and all participants can see it. When the trainer navigates through the document, moving from one page to another, the participants' screens follow along (see Figure 4–1).

Figure 4–1. Sharing Documents in Adobe Acrobat Connect Pro

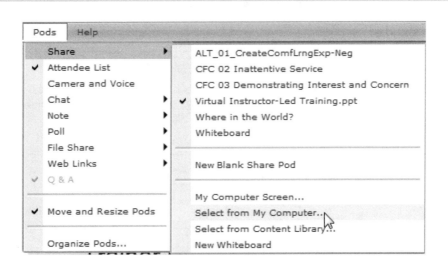

Source: Adobe® product screenshot reprinted with permission from Adobe Systems Incorporated

Common uses: Almost all virtual training classes use document sharing to display Microsoft Office PowerPoint slides. In addition, other documents, such as training manuals or pages from the class handout, also can be displayed.

Most programs can share Microsoft Office documents (Word, Excel, or PowerPoint), plus Portable Document Format (PDF) files. Some programs allow media files to be shared using this feature.

Unique characteristics: Some programs have participant privilege settings that give the participants free control over viewing the shared documents. This means they could move to a different slide than the one everyone else is viewing. Other programs give you control over whether or not participants can print the shared document. Check to see what privileges your attendees have for viewing shared documents.

Most virtual classroom software programs have a "Sync" or "Synchronize" command that can be used by the presenter to synchronize all participant screens. In other words, if participants are viewing different parts of a shared document, clicking on the Sync command will bring everyone together.

Check for file compatibility with the virtual classroom software: first, that the file type you wish to share can be uploaded, and second, that the version (such as Microsoft Office 2007 versus 2003) of the file you wish to upload is supported by the software.

Note that some virtual classroom software programs use the document-sharing feature to play audio or video files. In some programs, you simply open the media file as a shared document. Other programs require you to embed the media file into a PowerPoint slide using a proprietary add-in.

Chat. *Description:* Chat enables you to communicate with participants through real-time typed messages, similar to an instant messenger software program (see Figure 4–2). Chat messages can be public so that everyone sees the note, or sent privately to one individual user.

Private chat allows a participant to communicate directly with the host and/or the presenter. For example, I was delivering a virtual class and one of the participants sent me a private note explaining a personal reason why she wasn't able to complete an in-class assignment and requested that I please not call on her to share her answers to it.

Private chat also allows participants to chat with each other. For example, two participants in a training event could communicate with each other by sending messages back and forth in the chat window. In some virtual classroom programs,

Figure 4–2. Chat Window in Adobe Acrobat Connect Pro

Source: Adobe® product screenshot reprinted with permission from Adobe Systems Incorporated

this conversation would be completely private. Other programs allow the host to see all private conversations.

Common Uses: Chat enables you to engage participants during a training class in meaningful ways. The trainer can invite participants to send feedback, ask questions, and make comments during the program. The chat window can be a running commentary throughout the session.

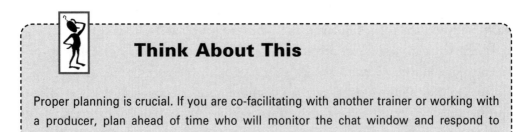

Think About This

Proper planning is crucial. If you are co-facilitating with another trainer or working with a producer, plan ahead of time who will monitor the chat window and respond to questions.

To increase participation during a discussion, a trainer could ask a question and direct participants to respond in the chat window. This method allows everyone to respond and get involved with the discussion.

The chat window can also be useful for the trainer to pass messages along to the participants during activities. For example, during a breakout session, the trainer can use the chat window to give timing reminders (such as "three minutes remaining" or "it's time to begin Round 2").

Think About This

Use all of your tools to communicate with participants and overcome any technical hang-ups. During one of my recent sessions, my telephone connection to the session unexpectedly dropped mid-sentence. I was still connected visually, just not verbally. So I typed a quick note in the chat area to let everyone know I was dialing right back in.

Private chat could also be used to create a "paired" discussion opportunity in class. Similar to a classroom session where a trainer says, "Turn to the person sitting next to you and discuss your response to this question," a trainer in the virtual classroom could direct participants to have a private chat.

Now, of course, private chat between participants opens up the possibility of them passing notes back and forth between each other, perhaps commenting about the training or their experience. While some trainers shy away from giving participants this type of control, I prefer to allow learners full access to the chat room and encourage them to communicate any way they wish.

Noted

I warn participants if you're going to talk about me or someone else in the class via private chat, make sure you're sending the message to the correct person before you click Send.
—Wendy Gates Corbett, Director, Education Services, Learn.com

Unique characteristics: Rules about private chat vary from program to program. In most programs, the host can choose whether or not private chat is allowed, and if it is allowed, whether participants can privately chat with each other (see Figure 4–3).

Figure 4–3. Participant Chat Privileges in Adobe Acrobat Connect Pro

Source: Adobe® product screenshot reprinted with permission from Adobe Systems Incorporated

If your participants include non-native language speakers, extra time may be needed for chatting answers. Some participants do not type as fast as others, which may also affect the timing of chat responses.

In one of my virtual training sessions, we play a trivia game on a topic related to the content and award points to the first person to correctly answer the question. Participants were directed to answer questions via chat. Interestingly, the first name that appeared on my chat window was not the first name on others' chat windows. So when I announced the winner, everyone erupted in protest. We discussed it and decided it was due to Internet bandwidth, although it could have also been user error on my part. We joked about it and turned it into a lighthearted event and learning experience, but it was a good lesson learned. In future sessions, I changed the directions and process for awarding points.

Annotate. *Description:* The annotation tools allow for real-time "drawing" on top of shared documents or a whiteboard. Annotation adds visual flair to your screen (see Figure 4–4). Annotation also focuses participant attention to specific areas of the screen.

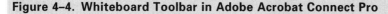
Figure 4–4. Whiteboard Toolbar in Adobe Acrobat Connect Pro

Source: Adobe® product screenshot reprinted with permission from Adobe Systems Incorporated

The exact annotation tools available vary from program to program. However, most allow you to

- draw lines and other shapes
- draw freehand with an electronic pencil or marker
- type text on the screen
- highlight words.

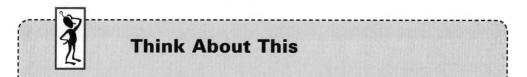

Think About This

A great virtual trainer should know all the tips and tricks of his or her preferred virtual classroom. Here's a quick tip that works in most software programs: To draw a perfectly straight line when using the "line" tool, hold down the Shift key while you draw it.

Common uses: The annotation tools help keep the screen visually interesting when the trainer "highlights" key words while speaking. For example, if the trainer displays a Microsoft Office PowerPoint slide with words, she would use the high-lighter annotation tool to select words of importance.

In most virtual classroom software programs, participants can be invited to annotate the screen. When they are able to draw or mark on the screen, it helps engage them into the learning content. For example, during a group brainstorm activity, the annotation's text tool can be used to add text to a slide or whiteboard (see Figure 4–5).

Unique characteristics: Check the participants' privileges to ensure they have (or can have) annotation rights. Some programs allow participants to annotate the screen if the option is selected. Other programs only allow presenters to annotate the screen.

Also learn how the eraser works. Find out who is able to erase what. Are you able to erase just your *own* annotations or *all* annotations? Find out the participants' privileges for erasing: Can they erase only their own annotations or all annotations? Are participants able to erase the presenter's annotations? If all annotations can be erased, be aware that this may affect one of your planned activities if someone accidentally erases all the marks on the screen.

Whiteboard. *Description:* A virtual whiteboard is similar to a classroom whiteboard or flipchart. It's a blank screen that can be typed, written, or drawn upon using the program's annotation tools.

Figure 4–5. Whiteboard Annotation Activity in Adobe Acrobat Connect Pro

Source: Adobe® product screenshot reprinted with permission from Adobe Systems Incorporated

Common uses: Whiteboards are used for brainstorming and other class activities that engage participants. Although the whiteboard screen starts as a blank page, the trainer can set it up ahead of time by adding drawings or other marks for an activity. For example, in one of my classes, we ask participants to brainstorm a SWOT analysis—Strengths, Weaknesses, Opportunities, and Threats—using a whiteboard exercise. Prior to the class, I use my own annotation tools to draw two lines to make the grid, and type in the labels: Strengths, Weaknesses, Opportunities, and Threats. At the appropriate time in class, participants are asked to type in suggestions on the screen.

Unique characteristics: Check to see how many whiteboards can be open or shared at one time. If you plan to use more than one, see if you can rename the whiteboard for easy reference during class.

Check the participants' privileges to ensure they have (or can have) annotation rights for the whiteboard. Also check to see if there are any limitations to how many participants can annotate at one time. In addition, be sure to find out how the eraser tool works for both the presenter and participants.

Polling. *Description:* Polls allow the trainer to ask survey questions in real time to participants. The questions can be multiple choice, multiple answer, or, in some programs, open ended.

Poll questions need to be initially created and then administered during the class. Creating a poll involves typing in the question and all possible responses. Administering the poll means sharing the poll at the correct time, opening it up for responses, closing the response window, and then sharing results with participants.

Common uses: Polls can be used to survey participants in an unlimited number of ways. In Figure 4–6, the trainer was delivering a class on adult learning techniques and had just finished an activity for the participants to discover their own preferred learning style. The trainer polled the class to find out their results.

Poll questions can also

▶ quiz participants' knowledge and understanding of a topic
▶ generate discussion using opinion questions
▶ solicit feedback from participants.

Unique characteristics: Some virtual classroom software programs allow for multiple questions in the same poll. Other programs limit each poll to one question only. Therefore, plan the sequence of your poll questions accordingly.

Figure 4–6. Sample Poll in Adobe Acrobat Connect Pro

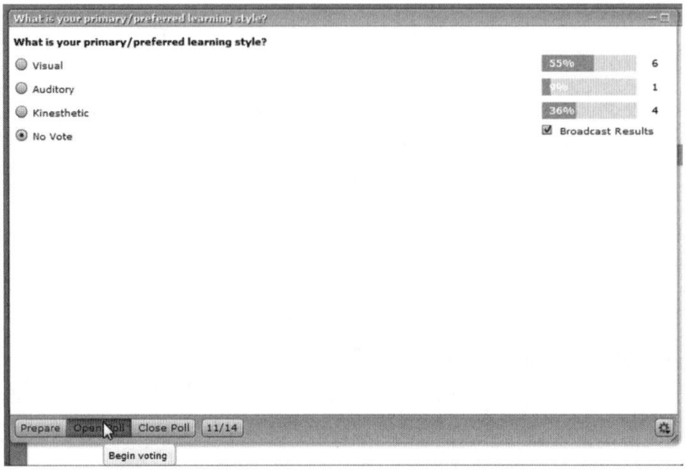

Source: Adobe® product screenshot reprinted with permission from Adobe Systems Incorporated

Some virtual classroom software programs allow you to create polls ahead of time and store them as separate files that can be uploaded to the classroom when needed. In other programs, you may need to type in the poll questions and answers as part of your day-of-class setup.

Raise Hand/Change Status. *Description:* Participants have the ability to communicate with the trainer by changing their status or raising their hand (see Figure 4–7). When someone clicks on this command, the trainer sees a small icon next to the participants' name indicating their status.

Common uses: This feature is often used for responding to closed-ended questions and quick yes/no polls. For example, a trainer might ask, "Who has seen this feature before? If you have, please 'raise your hand.'"

A trainer could also inform participants that raising their hands is one way to ask a question during class. When someone clicks on the "raise your hand" option, the trainer will call on him or her to speak.

In the virtual classroom software programs that offer more options than just raising your hand, this feature can also be used for more advanced polling. Participants can choose to agree or disagree with a statement, or respond "yes" or "no." This feature could also provide pacing feedback to the trainer (such as "speed up" or "slow down").

Figure 4–7. Raise Hand/Change Status Menu in Adobe Acrobat Connect Pro

Source: Adobe® product screenshot reprinted with permission from Adobe Systems Incorporated

Unique characteristics: In some programs, only the host and presenter can see the status change or "vote" of the participants. Other programs allow everyone to see the hand raised or status change.

Breakout Groups. *Description:* Breakout groups mimic small group activities in the face-to-face classroom (see Figure 4–8). If the trainer wants all participants to divide into smaller groups to complete a learning exercise such as a skills practice or brainstorm activity, then the trainer would assign participants to a breakout group. For example, a class with 15 participants might split into three teams of five people each.

In the virtual classroom, it's the same thing: The trainer would divide the class into smaller groups and then activate the breakouts. Participants move into a virtual private meeting room where they only hear their private conversation. They can share documents and whiteboards among themselves and collaborate together. The trainer has the ability to move in and out of the breakouts, just like he or she would walk around the room in a face-to-face session.

Common uses: Breakout groups can be used to practice skills learned during the training event. For example, if the class learns techniques for how to start a coaching conversation with an employee, the individuals could practice those techniques in a small group setting. In a practice breakout, one participant could practice the new coaching skill, another participant could be on the receiving end of the practice, and

Figure 4–8. Breakout Rooms in Adobe Acrobat Connect Pro

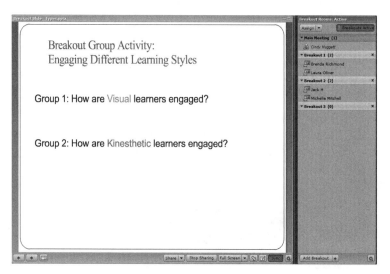

Source: Adobe® product screenshot reprinted with permission from Adobe Systems Incorporated

a third participant could be the silent observer. The participants could then rotate roles, each having a chance to practice the new coaching skill.

Another common use of breakouts is for small group brainstorming. Different groups could discuss different aspects of the same situation, or they could each discuss a different situation. You could even have the groups all discuss the same situation and then compare notes afterward.

In addition, any time you need to maximize participation, you might consider using breakout groups. These private collaboration sessions involve every participant because it's much tougher to "hide" in a small group. In other words, if you assign three participants to complete a group task versus assigning 15 participants to complete a group task, participants in the smaller group may be more likely to engage in the activity.

Unique characteristics: The audio choice in use during the virtual event will dictate how the audio functions in the breakout. In other words, if you are using the virtual classroom software's VoIP integrated audio, then when you create the breakout groups, the audio will automatically update. Participants in a small group will only be able to hear each other, as if they were on their own private line. However, if you use a separate conference calling line for the audio, then participants will need to manually move into their audio breakouts.

The number of breakout rooms available depends upon the virtual classroom software you're using. For example, Adobe Acrobat Connect Pro currently has a limit of five breakout rooms at one time.

On the conference call provider I use most, I sign into the conference call as the moderator and press *21 to activate the audio breakout groups. Then when it is time for participants to break out, they press # and their group number on the telephone. At the end of the activity, they press ## on their telephone to rejoin the main line. As the moderator, I can press #0 to "force" everyone back to the main group.

Application Sharing. *Description:* Application sharing allows trainers to open up their computer, specifically a certain software program, web browser, or desktop, to the participants (see Figure 4–9). Trainers select which application will be shared, and then participants will visually see it on their screen. When the trainer navigates through the program, participants follow along.

Figure 4–9. Menu Command to Access Desktop Sharing in Adobe Acrobat Connect Pro

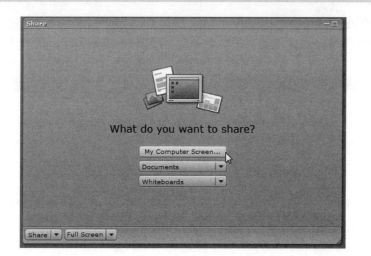

Source: Adobe® product screenshot reprinted with permission from Adobe Systems Incorporated

If the trainer shares her desktop, then the participants will view the trainer's computer, including all keyboard typing, mouse movements, and switching between programs. If the trainer shares a web browser, then the participants will see the trainer navigating the Internet. If the trainer shares a software program, then the participants will see just that one program.

The main difference between sharing your desktop and sharing just an application (either a software program or a web browser) is that when you choose to share your desktop, participants see everything. They will see your desktop's wallpaper, icons, and everything else you do on your computer. This feature can be useful if that's your goal. However, it is too revealing if you only want them to see one software program or just your web browser window.

A separate but related feature available in most virtual classroom programs is a shared remote control. A participant can be given control of the mouse pointer so that they can navigate and edit in the shared application. This can be useful during software training when you want a participant to gain hands-on experience with the program. The participant can use the remote control to practice a new skill learned. However, most programs only allow one person to be in control, so large classes might not benefit from taking turns one at a time.

Common uses: You could use application sharing when you need to display a file that is not supported by the virtual classroom program's document sharing. You could also use application sharing when you need to edit documents during class. For example, if you are demonstrating how to enter text into a file, then you would need to have the file open in editing mode, which is another way to think of application sharing. Perhaps the most common use of application sharing is when you are conducting software training in the virtual classroom. With application sharing, the software program becomes visible to all participants.

Unique characteristics: There is often a lag time between the time the trainer selects the "share application" or "share desktop" command and when the participants see the trainer's screen. During this pause, let participants know that it might take a few moments so that they don't think something is wrong with their screen.

Some virtual classroom software programs distinguish between desktop sharing, application sharing, and web browser sharing with separate tools for each. Other virtual classroom software programs combine these options into one command.

Noted

Become an expert on the software. You can't be an expert just by using it once a month. I used online meeting software for all my remote meetings, not just training. This forced me to really know the tool inside and out. . . . Great facilitators of in-person classes who do very few online facilitations just don't get comfortable enough with the software to transfer those great facilitation skills. You must know the tool. Attend all the training. Understand what every button does and when you would use it and when you would not. The biggest failure of online trainers is just not knowing the tool. It reflects badly on the course content and the experience.

—Mike Abrams, CEO, Resulting Idea, LLC

Getting It Done

It is critically important for you to know your software tools inside and out. A unique characteristic could be that the tool is only available under certain circumstances. For example, the annotation tools may not be visible to participants if they have not been granted privileges to use them. Or, the "assign breakout" command might only be available after you have clicked on a participant's name. Mastering your virtual classroom software means knowing every command and when each command can be used.

Mastering the software also means knowing it from the presenter's perspective and from the participant's perspective. The participant's screen will not look exactly the same as yours. For example, the participants may see a "raise hand" button, while the presenter sees a "make presenter" button in its place. As the host or presenter, you will often need to teach participants how the virtual classroom software works, and therefore, you need to know it from their point of view.

Finally, it's not enough to just read how tools work in an online help screen or user manual. You have to try them out yourself. There may be an undocumented quirk, or something about the feature that works in a way you didn't expect it to do so. Practice using the software so that you master it. Complete Worksheet 4–1 to determine which technology skills you want to learn more about.

Worksheet 4–1: Checklist for Learning Virtual Classroom Software

Use the following questions to organize your notes while learning a virtual classroom software program.

Name of virtual classroom software: _____

Which version? _____

Who is hosting the virtual classroom software?

Vendor	
Third party	
Other	

What sources of tech support for your virtual classroom software are available (such as via telephone, web, classes, dedicated tech support, and so on)?

_____

Use the following checklist to track your learning:

Feature	Unique Characteristics
Sharing Documents	
Chat	
Annotation	
Whiteboard	
Polling	
Raise Hand/Change Status	
Breakout Groups	
Application Sharing	

List other features here:	

Other notes about learning the software:

_____

_____

_____

5

Set Up for Success

░░░

What's Inside This Chapter

In this chapter, you'll learn

▶ How to prepare your virtual training classroom
▶ Computer, Internet, and telephone connection considerations
▶ Chronological steps to set up for success.

What's the first step to building a house? The foundation? The cornerstone? The basement? No! The first step to building a house is the planning—creating a blueprint for the final design. The successful completion of a finished house depends largely on how well it was planned.

The same holds true for virtual training. The success of your class will largely depend upon how well you have prepared. Setting up for success must be done in advance of classes you deliver—every class, every time.

In many ways, setting up for a successful virtual class is similar to setting up for a face-to-face class. You prepare your notes, double check the logistics, and find out about the participants. You arrive at the training location early to arrange the room appropriately and set up your equipment. You get your glass of water, put on a smile, and greet participants as they arrive.

It's exactly the same with virtual training. You prepare your notes, double check the logistics, and find out about the participants. You also need to set up your equipment and arrive early to prepare the online classroom.

Preparing Your Virtual Classroom

Of course, since the delivery method of virtual training is different, your set-up routine will naturally be different. You'll be setting up your computer and the virtual software instead of a physical classroom. You have different communication tools that need to be tested and ready to go. Your delivery workspace is usually your office, which needs to be prepared for training instead of your regular working routine.

Noted

The learners want you to be successful.

—Wendy Gates Corbett, Director, Education Services, Learn.com

In both the face-to-face environment and the virtual one, the amount of time you spend preparing is probably equal to or more than the amount of time you spend in the class. You have to learn the content, get ready to deliver it, and ensure the class will meet the intended outcomes. An experienced virtual trainer would probably spend the same amount of preparation time as an experienced classroom trainer would take to prepare for a face-to-face class. However, you should heed Bob Pike's classic advice from *Creative Training Techniques*: "Proper preparation . . . prevents poor performance." This advice magnifies in virtual training delivery. There is less room for error because of the technology and the lack of visual connection with participants.

In addition to the event-specific preparation that classroom trainers do for each training class, there are also some general virtual training preparation steps. For example, classroom trainers create a training supply kit and replenish it when needed. They keep their skills fresh by attending professional development programs. These types of general preparation steps are also necessary for virtual trainers.

Let's begin with the general steps needed for virtual trainers to set up for success. These steps are not necessarily time sensitive or associated with a specific class. They are general things you should do to set up for virtual training delivery.

Your three primary tools for virtual delivery are your computer, Internet connection, and telephone (unless you are using VoIP). Each one needs to be carefully considered in your virtual training setup.

Computer, Internet, and Telephone Considerations

Computer. With the multitude of computer choices on the market, does it matter what kind you use for virtual training delivery? Yes and no. Whether it's a laptop, desktop, or netbook, as long as it meets the minimum technology requirements for your virtual classroom software, then it will be fine. You should also ensure the computer has all necessary software and accessories for your class. For example, if you plan to use audio-visual media during the session, be sure you have a sound card and speakers.

You may have personal preferences, such as a full-size keyboard or a regular mouse instead of a laptop's touchpad, so you should select the types of tools that are most comfortable for you.

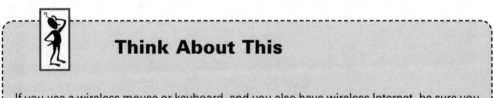

Think About This

If you use a wireless mouse or keyboard, and you also have wireless Internet, be sure you test them out to ensure there's no interference. Some wireless frequencies can interfere with each other.

If you use an ultra-portable laptop or netbook, be aware that its small size may prevent you from seeing the screen clearly. This limitation could affect the quality of your training delivery. For example, if you miss seeing someone's hand raised because of the tiny icon on your small screen, a participant's question might go unanswered.

Recent technology innovations allow us to use smartphones in place of full-size computers for browsing the Internet. A smartphone is a telephone with data capability. It has a keyboard for typing (either a physical one or on the screen) and mouse or touchpad technology. It can browse the Internet. The line is blurring between laptops, netbooks, and smartphones in terms of functionality and power. While it is possible to use some smartphones to connect to a virtual training event, it is not yet an ideal solution for the host or trainer.

For example, some virtual classroom software programs can run on smartphones. However, at the time of this writing, most do not yet support presenter privileges and therefore cannot be used to fully facilitate a virtual training event. There are workarounds, such as starting the meeting as the host and allowing someone else to present. Unfortunately, that would be like a trainer trying to conduct a face-to-face class from a remote location over a conference phone. Someone onsite would press Play on the DVD and turn the flipchart pages. While it's possible to do that in a pinch, it's not the way you would want to run a training class. So, technically it may be possible to deliver virtual training using a smartphone, but it should not be your first choice.

Computer Contingency Planning

When delivering a virtual class, you should have two computers on your desk. The first computer is your main terminal. Use it to log in as the host or presenter (depending upon which role and which software you are using). Ensure that all of the files you need, including your shared documents, are available to you on this computer.

The second computer is what you use to log in to the class as a participant. You don't actively use this computer during the class. Instead, you should glance at it periodically, like you would a sideview mirror when driving. This computer will show you what the participants are seeing at any given time. This is important to do because your presenter screen will not look exactly the same as the participant screen.

Wendy Gates Corbett, Director of Education Services at Learn.com, calls this second computer her "sidekick" because it sits side by side her main computer on her desk (see Figure 5–1).

Another benefit to having a second computer is the extra insurance it provides. Should your main computer unexpectedly crash or have connection difficulties, the second computer could become your main one. Because it's right there on your desk, already powered and ready to go, it would be a quick transition.

Speaking of "extra insurance," part of your overall computer setup for virtual delivery should include contingency planning. You should consider ahead of time what you would do if your computer unexpectedly stopped working.

Figure 5–1. Wendy Gates Corbett's Computer and Sidekick

Basic Rule 9

Have at least one back-up plan for equipment technology. You never know when you might need to use it.

Having the second "sidekick" computer is one recommended back-up option. If a third computer could be available, even better! You might easily have access to a third computer if you work in an office environment. If you work from home, you might have alternatives within your family, a neighbor, or even a nearby public computer lab (if it's a quiet environment!). Regardless of the options immediately available to you, take some time to think about what alternatives you could use when needed.

However, your computer back-up plans shouldn't stop there. If you needed to quickly switch to another computer, make sure it would be ready for you to use it right away. For example, if your virtual classroom software requires plug-ins, download them ahead of time just in case. Have a second copy of your training files already loaded onto the back-up computer, or at least onto a portable USB thumb drive. Your secondary computer choice should be 100 percent prepared, as if it was going to be your primary computer.

Internet Connection. The second necessity for successful virtual delivery is a reliable Internet connection. Without question, you should have high-speed connectivity. Although it's possible to use the Internet via dial-up modem, you do not want to have the slowest connection of the class. Your setup should not detract from the training in any way, which could result from a slow Internet connection.

If you're working from an office location, the Internet speed should not be a factor because most corporate offices have fast connections. If for any reason your work environment does not have a high-speed connection, find another location, such as a public wi-fi hotspot, from which to deliver your training.

The choice of wired or wireless Internet is not as important as the reliability of your connection. If you normally use wireless Internet but do not have a strong, steady signal, then change to a more dependable wired connection.

There are times you may need to deliver a virtual training session from a remote location—somewhere other than your usual spot. For example, you may be traveling and need to facilitate training from your hotel room or airport. Once again, as long as you have a strong, steady, reliable Internet connection, your physical location should not matter. (Of course, if you are in a public location, ensure the background noise will not distract from your delivery.)

Internet Contingency Planning

When setting up for your virtual training sessions, create back-up plans for connecting to the Internet. Just like having a spare computer is essential, knowing where else you could quickly find an Internet connection is also important. Ask yourself, "What would I do if I lost Internet connectivity just prior to or during a session?"

Once again, if you work in a corporate office environment, the reliability of your Internet connection will probably not be an issue. However, it is still a good idea to know if there is a neighboring office building or public wi-fi hotspot nearby. If you frequently deliver virtual training, consider having a back-up Internet option, such as a broadband wireless card through a cellular service provider.

Another part of your preparation should be to create a back-up plan for what to do if you don't have Internet at all. A few possibilities are to

- coordinate with your producer or co-facilitator to have them run the session
- use a smartphone to connect (if your virtual classroom software program supports it) and ask someone else to navigate the screen
- reschedule the session for another time.

None of these options are ideal, so remember to plan additional Internet possibilities. With the abundance of wireless and cellular Internet options available in most geographic locations, this extra planning should be a standard part of your virtual delivery setup.

Basic Rule 10
Use a strong, reliable Internet connection and a crystal-clear telephone line.

Telephone Connection. As we discussed in chapter 3, unless you plan to use the virtual classroom software's VoIP capabilities, you will need a telephone for the audio connection.

Whether you work in a business environment or in a home office, you will most likely have a telephone and handset at your desk. You probably also have a cell phone you could use. And, if you plan to deliver from a conference room in an office, you may also have a conference room-style speakerphone.

With all of these choices, which one should you use to deliver virtual training? Similar to your Internet choice, your telephone selection is not as important as the clarity of its sound. The connection should be strong, reliable, and crystal clear. That means if you normally use a cell phone but occasionally experience dropped calls or have a weak signal, use a landline.

Since you need to use your hands for typing on the keyboard and clicking with the mouse, you should have a hands-free telephone setup. However, do not use a speakerphone because of the potential for echo and background noise.

Use a cordless telephone when possible. It gives you the ability to get up and move around while facilitating. Joe Willmore, President and Founder of Willmore Consulting Group, also recommends using a cordless telephone because if a participant asks a question, instead of writing it down and saying he'll get back to them, he can walk over to his bookshelf and look up the answer.

Also, some trainers like to stand while talking so there's more energy in their voice. A cordless telephone gives you the freedom and flexibility to do this.

However, be aware that some cordless phones might interfere with a wireless Internet connection due to the competing frequencies. Be sure to test your setup well in advance of your training delivery.

For my hands-free connection, I use a cordless telephone with a wired headset connected to the handset. I am able to stand up and move around if needed. The wired headset has a headband, earphone, and extended microphone. It also has adjustable volume and a mute button. I prefer a wired headset because it minimizes any potential for electronic interference.

Telephone Contingency Planning

Not only should you have contingency plans for your computer and your Internet connection, you should also have a back-up plan for your audio connection. Consider all of your alternatives for audio connectivity. For example: If your telephone equipment stopped working, what nearby telephone could you easily access? Do you have another cordless handset? Do you have more than one telephone connection option, such as a landline and a cell phone?

   ▸ *Tip:* For each primary and back-up telephone you plan to use, make sure each one is fully charged prior to the event
   ▸ *Tip:* Make sure all of your cords are plugged in securely to all outlets, receptacles, and equipment. Also make sure the cords are not in the way and will not be potential hazards to trip over in case you stand up or move.

Setting Up for Success

Now that you have secured the basics for virtual delivery, let's look in chronological order at all the other steps involved with setting up for success.

Two Weeks Prior to Class. Approximately two weeks prior to your virtual training event, you should have all of the logistics set and materials prepared.

First, regardless of who sets up the administrative details of your event, you should have all logistical information at least two weeks prior to the class. This information includes

- course information (class name, instructor notes, participant information, and so on)
- virtual classroom event website link (including all passcodes)
- conference call numbers and passcodes (for both the moderator/host and for the participants).

It is a misperception that virtual events can be organized closer to the delivery date because details can be communicated quickly via email. The reality is that all logistics should be planned and communicated well in advance. It *is* important to send email or other reminders prior to the session; however, these reminders should not take the place of initial communication.

If your organization uses scheduling software like Microsoft Office Outlook or Lotus Notes, put logistical details in the calendar request. The event appointment should contain all website links, telephone numbers, passcodes, and any prerequisite material that is needed for class. In my experience, participants who receive an official meeting request to hold the time on their calendar will also look to that electronic appointment reminder for the connection details. Having all of the details in that one location will minimize the need for participants to search for the information just prior to the class start time.

Second, around this time you should prepare all necessary class materials. The materials include the content, your facilitator guide, any virtual classroom activities that need advance preparation, and all participant materials.

The first time you deliver a class, you need to both learn the material and prepare your training notes. You may have a formal facilitator guide to follow, or maybe just an informal text file with notes. The format of facilitator guides varies depending upon its source. If you wear multiple hats, such as instructional designer and trainer, then you may even design your own facilitator guide.

This is not a book on instructional design; however, if you design your own training material and need to create training notes for virtual delivery, I recommend using a table-type format similar to Table 5–1.

Table 5–1. Sample Format for Facilitator Notes

Time	Producer Notes	Tools to Use	Facilitator Notes

Even if this is the 50th time you have delivered the same class, you should prepare your training notes every time. The same class for you will be a new class for your learners. Each audience has unique needs, and so you should not only remind yourself of the class material, you should also tailor your content to the group. For example, the stories you share may need to be updated, or the questions you ask might be in a new context.

As you learn about the needs of your learners, you can find out their lingo and incorporate it into your notes. Maybe they refer to themselves as "associates" instead of "employees," or they have "supervisors" instead of "managers." These small details will help you better connect with your audience and enhance their learning experience.

Every trainer has his or her own way to specifically prepare the facilitator guide. Some write all over their guide with circles, underlines, stars, highlights, and other identifying marks. Others use sticky notes on the guide pages so they can change their notes for each class. There is no one right way to prepare your facilitator guide. What's important is that you can follow it during the class as you intended.

My personal preference for facilitator guide preparation is to print all materials (mine are usually in electronic format). I highlight all of the key words in the guide, and write notes in big bold print so that I don't miss anything. I occasionally place small sticky notes strategically in the guide to hold stories or promptings. I use tape flags to mark sections of the guide and any important reference pages.

I also print all participant materials, and a six-slide-per-page handout version of my Microsoft Office PowerPoint slides. On the handout, I write a brief description of what should be happening in the class just before that slide is displayed. For example, if we will use a whiteboard activity, I'll write "whiteboard" or if we will use a specific poll question, I'll write "poll #3." This handout document serves as my "big-picture" view of the class and becomes one of my back-up plans should anything happen to my trainer notes.

In addition, I use a manila file folder to hold my papers for each class. I write the connection information for the host and participants on the inside front cover. I also put a large ruled sticky note on the inside front cover with a checklist of everything I need to do to prepare the virtual classroom (such as polls to upload, attendee privileges to check, whiteboards to share and rename, and so on). Inside the folder is a copy of the participant list, all emergency contact information, my facilitator notes, and the participant materials.

Think About This

If you print your own virtual training facilitator guide, use a laser printer instead of ink-jet so that you can highlight the pages without smudging ink.

Third, if you are new or relatively new to virtual delivery, you should be practicing your facilitation skills using the virtual classroom software at least two weeks (or more) prior to the event. Don't wait until the last minute to begin practicing. We'll cover more information about practicing in chapter 9.

One Week Prior to Class. Approximately one week prior to the class, you should be working with your producer or co-facilitator (if you have one) to solidify all delivery details. Take time to figure out exactly when and how presenter handoffs will occur during the session. Determine who will take responsibility for which parts of the program, and who will "drive" the software tools. For example, if one person will use the annotation tools to highlight words on the slide while the other person is talking, agree on what words will be highlighted and when. Or, if a participant question appears in the chat window, decide ahead of time how and when the person with chat moderator responsibilities will interrupt the speaker.

Also, if you are working with a producer or co-facilitator, decide on a way for you to communicate outside of the virtual classroom software. For example, will you be able to text one another via cell phone during the class or will you have a separate instant messenger program available? This back-up communication option might come in handy during emergency situations either before or during the class.

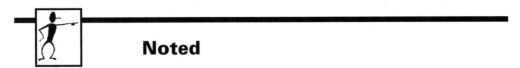

Noted

My co-facilitator had to work from home with a sick child and possibly step away to deal with a medical emergency. We worked out if one wasn't there, the other would immediately step in and cover, making it seamless for the participants.

—Joe Willmore, President and Founder, Willmore Consulting Group

In addition, a few business days before the training, participants should receive reminder messages about the program. If you—the trainer—are responsible for this, then put a note in your calendar tickler file or to-do list to send out these reminders.

Think About This

Check the calendar to see if any holidays fall close to your training event. If so, anticipate that some participants may be out on vacation around that time and send reminders well in advance.

Finally, if you are using a virtual classroom software program that allows you to set up the "room" in advance, go ahead and prepare it at least three business days prior to the event. While three days may seem like excess time, it will allow your room to be prepared and give you extra cushion—just in case your time gets filled with illness or some other unexpected calamity.

Day Before the Class. The day before your class, you should double check all critical training details. These include

- ▶ reviewing the class roster/participant list for any last minute changes or additions
- ▶ reviewing your training notes one last time
- ▶ reviewing your back-up contingency plans
- ▶ charging all electronic equipment.

You should also double check the class time and time zones. Joe Willmore tells the story of how he had a virtual training event scheduled on his calendar in Eastern Standard Time. However, he was out of town that week, and happened to be in the Central Standard Time zone. The time on his calendar was one hour different than the event time. He realized his mistake a few minutes before the event was to begin. Fortunately, his producer was already online with the participants, and Joe was able to log in just in time for the event. His lesson learned? To always double and triple check the time and time zone for each event.

In addition, the day before the class, participants should receive one final reminder about the training event. To make it interesting, and not just another reminder, provide a brainteaser or interesting statistic related to the course content along with the reminder. This will help get your participants thinking about the topic and prepared to learn.

Day of Class. Your day-of-training routine will vary depending upon what time of day the event is scheduled. With virtual training, it could be scheduled for any time of day depending upon where your participants are located. I've delivered virtual training at 7 a.m. and at 10 p.m. to accommodate international participants in different time zones. Therefore, "day of class" means the day of the event, a few hours prior to it.

First, set up your workspace for the training event. Clear your desk of everything except what you'll need to deliver virtually. Make sure your notes are organized and everything is where you want it to be. Have your class roster accessible on your desk, along with a pen or pencil to mark on it. I also find it helpful to have a notepad nearby in case I need to jot down a note during class. Also have all of the connection details—the weblinks, conference call numbers, and all passcodes—written down or printed out on paper on your desk. This way, if you lose Internet connectivity or your computer unexpectedly does not work, you have all of the connection information immediately available.

▶ *Tip from Wendy Gates Corbett:* Always reboot your computer prior to your virtual training delivery. While it may not be technically necessary to do this, it helps close down any open files and gives you a fresh start.

You should be in a room by yourself for your training delivery. This is important to minimize any background noise or conversations. For example, you would not want to deliver virtually from a cubicle office environment. The potential for disruption, from loud conversations in the background to someone walking into your workspace, is just too great.

Think About This

Some trainers who work in an open space or cubicle environment find it is difficult to locate an empty, enclosed room in their office location to deliver training. If this is a problem for you, get creative to explore alternative delivery spaces. You could consider

- working from a home office on days you deliver virtual training
- creating a designated virtual training delivery room in your office building
- borrowing someone else's office for training delivery.

Also, you should not have any participants in the room with you—even if it's a large conference room. You should not try to present both online and in person at the same time. Your focus is divided between the groups, and you will subconsciously favor one group over the other. It will be a very subtle difference, barely noticeable by most, but it will still have impact. For example, you might say something like, "As you can see here . . . " referring to something that only the in-person group can see. Or when you call on participants by name, you may use the names from the participant list disproportionately because you see them in writing on your screen. Therefore, when setting up your workspace, make it a private one.

Next, check the power levels of your electronic equipment. Even if you charged them up the day before or overnight, check again to ensure they have full battery power available.

Noted

Even if your computer could run on battery power during your delivery, use it plugged in. Why? In case you lose power, you'll still have "juice" to keep going.

—Joe Willmore, President and Founder, Willmore Consulting Group

You should also take care of your personal needs starting a few hours prior to the event. For example, find a middle ground between an empty and a full stomach. You don't want to be distracted by hunger but also not overly full and uncomfortable. Use the bathroom so that you don't have to step away from the computer during your session, and limit your liquid intake to a level that works for you.

Also set a bottle of room temperature water near your workspace. If necessary, go ahead and crack open the bottle's seal, but leave it covered to protect from any spills. If you prefer a glass, find one with a lid or use a plastic wrap covering.

If you work in an office environment and plan to use a conference room for delivery, when reserving the room be sure to start your room reservation at least one hour before your session begins. For example, if your virtual training session begins at 10 a.m., then reserve the conference room starting at 9 a.m. This scheduling tactic will give you enough time to get into the room for set up without any scheduling conflicts.

If you work from home, make plans for your pets, children, or other family members who might disturb you during your session. You might close off an area of the house for pets to stay during your virtual deliveries, so that no unexpected dog barking in the background disrupts your class. While your dog may normally be a quiet companion, the doorbell may ring and result in barking. A separate pet space—away from your workspace—will also prevent cats from jumping up onto your keyboard during the session. For other people in your house, you could alert them to your training schedule and make a Do Not Disturb sign for the door as a reminder.

If you're on the road and delivering virtually from a hotel room, place the hotel's Do Not Disturb sign on your door so that you will not be interrupted.

In my home office, I close the door before a virtual training class. I also keep a cat toy in my desk drawer. In the unlikely event that my door unexpectedly opens by a family member and my cat wanders in the room, I can quickly reach for the toy and toss it out into the hallway, which distracts my cat and gives me a chance to close the door.

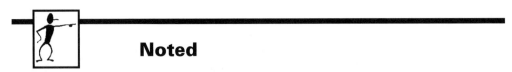

Noted

My son made a sign for my home office door. It says "Do Not Enter: Virtual Classroom in Session."

—Tracy Stallard, Training Performance Consultant, AchieveGlobal

One Hour Before Class. One hour before class is "showtime" in my book. I log in to the virtual classroom approximately 45–60 minutes prior to a session. Although this may seem early, this extra time gives me a chance to check all technology connections and make sure everything is working as it should. If I'm using a time-specific virtual classroom software, then I'll also use this time to set the classroom: sharing documents, loading poll questions, opening whiteboards, and checking participant privileges. My goal is to be ready for delivery at least 30 minutes before the session begins. If you are using the recommended "sidekick" computer, go ahead and log it in to the virtual classroom as well.

If working with a producer who will handle the technology setup, then I log in approximately 30–35 minutes prior to the class start time. I want to be online and settled before any participants arrive.

Fifteen Minutes Before Class. Dial into the conference calling software, take a deep breath, and have fun!

Noted

I have a whiteboard over my desk with key thoughts and themes on it. It's my "centering" and my focal point. My key thoughts include "Breathe," "Be Calm," "Talk at a normal pace," "You are the expert," "Have fun," "They're here to learn." I also post key themes of the class, and a few story ideas. That way, if something goes wrong and I need to fill time, I have an immediate story to tell. There are times I never look at it, and times I need it."

—Jeff Smith, Senior Consultant, The Titan Group

Getting It Done

The more prepared you are for your virtual delivery, the more relaxed you will be. You'll have confidence in your equipment, in your knowledge of the content, in your comfort with the technology, and in your readiness to deliver. Do not overlook the importance of your preparation. Build in enough time to fully prepare for the training. Set yourself up for success.

Use the checklist in Worksheet 5–1 to ensure you are "extra prepared" for virtual delivery.

Worksheet 5–1: The Extra Prepared Virtual Trainer Checklist

Place a checkmark next to the items that are completely true for you. Then add up the number of checks in each section, totaling all checks for a final score. You will find the scoring key at the end.

Virtual Classroom Software

	I know the full extent of the virtual classroom software's capabilities.
	When logged in as the host, I know what every button and every menu command does.
	When logged in as the presenter, I know what every button and every menu command does.
	When logged in as a participant, I know what every button and every menu command does.
	I am aware of all unique features of the virtual classroom software (for example, how many breakout groups can be used at one time).
	I know what file types are supported by the virtual classroom software's file sharing feature.
	I have tested every feature and activity that we will be using in the virtual classroom during my training event.
	Subtotal

Internet

	I have a solid high-speed Internet connection in the location where I will be delivering virtual training.
	I have a back-up Internet connection available in the location where I will be delivering virtual training.
	I have a second back-up Internet connection available in the location where I will be delivering virtual training.
	I have an alternate location that has a solid high-speed Internet connection that I can quickly get to at the last minute.
	I have a second alternate location that has a solid high-speed Internet connection that I can quickly get to at the last minute.
	Subtotal

Computer

	I have a reliable computer or laptop that I will use to deliver virtual training.
	I have a second reliable computer or laptop that I will use as a "sidekick" when delivering virtual training.
	I have another back-up reliable computer or laptop that I can use as my main or sidekick computer to deliver virtual training.
	I have one more back-up reliable computer or laptop that I can use as my main or sidekick computer to deliver virtual training.
	All software, drivers, and plug-ins necessary to deliver virtual training are fully installed on all of my primary and back-up computers.
	All of my back-up computers are powered on and ready to go prior to the start time of my virtual training event.
	All of my back-up computers are fully charged and can run from battery power if needed.
	Subtotal

Telephony

	I have reliable telephone service that I will use when delivering virtual training.
	I have a back-up telephone connection that can be used if needed (i.e., my main telephone is a landline and my back-up telephone is a cell phone).
	I have a second back-up telephone connection that can be used if needed (i.e., my main telephone is a landline, my back-up telephone is a cell phone, and my second backup uses a different cell service provider).
	I have a compatible hands-free headset to use with my telephone.
	I have a back-up compatible hands-free headset to use with my telephone.
	I have additional compatible hands-free headset to use with each back-up telephone.
	My telephone, and all accessories I use, have a clear sound connection (i.e., I can be clearly heard at all times when speaking).
	All back-up telephones and accessories have a clear sound connection (i.e., I can be clearly heard at all times when speaking).
	My primary telephone handset is fully charged prior to the start of the virtual training event.
	All of my back-up telephones are fully charged prior to the start of the virtual training event.
	Subtotal

Training Files

	I have a printed copy of every training file associated with the virtual training event (facilitator guide, participant workbook, saved poll questions, and so on).
	I have a second printed copy of every training file associated with the virtual training event.
	I have a third printed copy of every training file associated with the virtual training event.
	I have an electronic copy of every training file associated with the virtual training event that can be easily accessed on my computer's hard drive.
	I have an electronic copy of every training file associated with the virtual training event that can be easily accessed on every *back-up* computer's hard drive.
	I have an electronic copy of every training file associated with the virtual training event that can be easily accessed on a portable drive (such as a USB drive or portable hard drive).
	I have an electronic copy of every training file associated with the virtual training event that can be easily accessed from any computer with an Internet connection (i.e., stored on an accessible website).
	Subtotal

Training Event

	I have all web links for my virtual training event, including host, presenter, and participant links if they are different.
	I have all event passcodes, including host, presenter, and participant codes if they are different.
	I have all teleconference details, including moderator and participant codes.
	I know all of the teleconference commands for moderators (for example, *21 to activate breakout groups).
	I know all of the teleconference participant commands (for example, *6 to mute and *7 to unmute an individual telephone line).
	I have all logistical details, including web links, passcodes, and teleconference information, printed out prior to the virtual training event.
	Subtotal

Facilitator Support

	I have a producer who will assist with all technical details of the virtual training event.
	I have a back-up producer who could fill in for the producer if needed.
	I have a second back-up producer who could fill in if needed.
	I have another facilitator or trainer who could fill in for me at the last minute if needed.
	I have a second back-up facilitator or trainer who could fill in for me at the last minute if needed.
	I have a technology specialist available to assist participants behind the scenes.
	I have operator support for the teleconferencing service (if used).
	A technical support person who is knowledgeable of the virtual classroom software and teleconference service is on-site and available at every location from which participants will be dialing in.
	Subtotal

And . . . since this is an "extra prepared" checklist, here's a bonus section.

Participants

	I know the participants' full names and job positions prior to the virtual training event.
	I know the length of time each participant has been with his or her organization.
	I know the length of time each participant has been in his or her current role.
	I know the biggest challenge(s) the participants have related to the training topic.
	I know the "burning questions" that participants will have related to the training topic.
	I know whether or not each participant has talked with his or her direct supervisor about the training topic.
	I know whether or not participants will be held accountable for the new learning.
	I have personally spoken to each participant about the training event.
	I have verified that each participant has completed all prerequisite courses for the training topic.
	I have verified that each participant has completed all pre-work for the training event.
	Subtotal
	Grand Total

Scoring Key

60	Fantastic! Enter your name on the Extra Prepared Trainer All-Star List!
50–59	Excellent! Very well done. Consider helping other trainers learn from your preparation efforts.
40–49	Congratulations! You are extra-prepared to deliver virtual training.
30–39	You are prepared, but have room for improvement. Select a few areas where you can improve your preparation.
20–29	You are on the verge of preparation. Identify the next five items you can add to your virtual delivery preparation.
10–19	You have started to prepare and have an opportunity to improve. Select 10 items from this checklist that are most important for you, and make an effort to add those to your list.
0–9	Ask an experienced virtual trainer for assistance in getting started.

6

Get Really Good
at Multitasking

■■

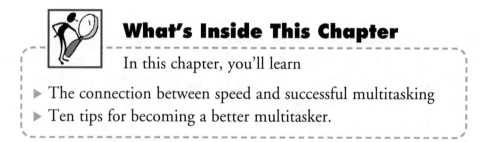

What's Inside This Chapter

In this chapter, you'll learn

▶ The connection between speed and successful multitasking
▶ Ten tips for becoming a better multitasker.

In many ways, multitasking in the virtual classroom is like driving a car. When you drive, you need to keep your eyes focused straight ahead on the road. Yet, you use your peripheral vision to watch for unexpected changes. You frequently glance in your rearview mirror and check your side mirrors as well. You are also pressing down the gas pedal, steering the car, watching your speed, and listening to the radio. In addition, you may adjust the temperature, switch radio channels, or turn on your windshield wipers. And let's not forget that you are looking at street signs, stopping at signal lights, and paying attention to pedestrians and the other drivers around you. You may also be chatting with the passengers in your car. If something goes wrong, like a dashboard warning light appearing, you manage the situation, taking precautions to remedy it. And all the while, you're driving with a destination in mind and moving toward it. Getting to your final destination is dependent upon your car and your ability to drive it.

When you first learned how to drive, remembering to do all of those things at once was a challenge. You had to practice and practice and practice some more. You probably had a learner's permit, took driving lessons, and needed an escort in the car with you. You may have been able to drive during daytime hours only at first, and then gradually added in night-time driving once you gained more experience.

It will be the same in the virtual classroom. At first, it may seem like everything is coming at you at once, and there are so many steps to remember. You have to manage the technology and keep your eyes on the main screen, but also remember to check the chat window, the participant list, your facilitator notes, and your side-kick computer. You need to prepare for the next activity while keeping everyone's focus and attention on the current one. You have to watch the clock and remember to engage the participants.

Rest assured that like driving, multitasking in the virtual classroom will get easier over time. After learning the software, understanding technology, practicing your delivery techniques, and perhaps even working with a more experienced virtual trainer, you will master the multitasking required to be effective. With practice, it will eventually feel like second nature.

The Connection Between Speed and Multitasking

Another way to think about multitasking is to consider the way your computer works. If you have multiple programs open on your computer desktop simultaneously—an Internet browser, your email program, a word processing program, an instant messenger, and so on—it seems as if the computer handles all these things at once. In reality, the computer processor can only take one command at a time. It just seems to handle them all at once because of the speed at which the commands are processed. The faster the processor speed, the faster the computer works.

Our human brain is often compared to a computer processor. Our brain processes commands, thoughts, tasks, and other complex information. Like the computer, we are seemingly able to process many things at once. Whether we process simultaneously or one thought at a time, it is the *speed* at which we're able to process information and complete tasks that is important to our success at multitasking. If you can speed up, then you will to improve your ability to multitask.

I believe it is possible to learn to speed up and therefore increase your multitasking skills. Of course, speed is one, but not the only, significant factor in successful multitasking. Let's look at all the ways you can learn to be a better multitasker.

Think About This

Some people seem to naturally be better at multitasking than others. It's as if they can balance more than one thing at a time and they make it look easy. Meanwhile, other people can only concentrate on what's in front of them at the moment. If there's too much going on at once, they feel overloaded and overwhelmed.

Some people prefer a fast-paced environment. They constantly move from one thing to the next, often doing more than one thing at a time. Multitasking seems natural to them. However, many other people prefer a slower pace. They focus on one task, and then the next.

Neither method is better than the other. It's simply something to be aware of in yourself. Do you prefer a fast- or slow-paced environment? As you go about your work over the next few days, pay attention to your preferred style. Do you quickly move between tasks with multiple things going on at once, or do you prefer to focus on just one thing at a time? Knowing your preference will help you know ahead of time how you might react to multitasking in the virtual classroom.

How to Multitask

First, if you follow the other steps in this book, you will automatically be a better multitasker. When you are prepared, know the software, practice, and set yourself up for success, you will be able to concentrate on everything else that needs to be done while delivering your presentation.

On the other hand, if you are not quite comfortable with the technology, or you try to "wing it" with the material, you will simply add to your stress level and likely have more difficulty. You will suffer at the hand of all the "things" you need to do to be an effective virtual trainer.

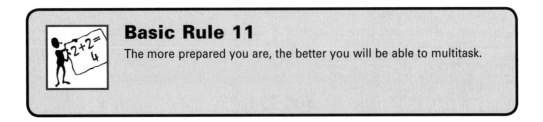

Basic Rule 11
The more prepared you are, the better you will be able to multitask.

I recommend the following 10 specific things to help you get really good at multitasking in the virtual classroom. Some of these tips will enable you to quicken your processing speed; others will help you be a more effective multitasker.

1. Set up for success.
2. Be prepared with content.
3. Know your virtual classroom software program.
4. Have a producer or co-facilitator.
5. Be a proficient typist.
6. Build in pauses to regroup.
7. Practice multitasking.
8. Remember how you do it in the face-to-face classroom.
9. Resist temptation to do too much.
10. Know what's OK to let slide.

Set Up for Success. One reason you are able to multitask successfully when driving is because you know where to consistently find everything on the console and dashboard. The same should be true when you deliver in the virtual classroom. You should be able to mentally picture every item in your workspace and be able to reach for it without much thought. You should also know where to find everything on your computer screen. The goal is to be able to do things without having to stop and concentrate on them.

To help you meet this goal, set up your workspace for maximum efficiency. Clean your desk so that it's neat and organized. Have your trainer notes and other papers in order, clipped together so they stay in place. If possible, use a swivel chair on wheels so you can move and turn easily. When everything is organized, you won't need to worry about where things are or how to reach them.

Set up your workspace the same way for every class. You may need to experiment a few times to see what specific setup works best for you. This consistent setup will start to feel comfortable and natural, which will help you multitask.

Think About This

Comfort, organization, and consistency are key in setting up your workspace. For my own setup, I write with my left hand, so I place my laptop on the right side of my desk toward the back. My telephone is tucked in beside the laptop. My trainer notes are on the left side of the laptop, with the handout perched on a stand. My sidekick computer is on the far right side of my desk turned sideways for easy viewing. I also have a small table next to my desk with back-up notes, files, and accessories.

When your workspace is set up appropriately, with everything you need in reach, you will be able to automate your workflow. It will be a breeze to reach for what you need when you need it, which, in turn, will help you move faster and be more efficient. Speed in movement helps you multitask.

Be Prepared with Content. You should know your training material and content so well that you could facilitate in your sleep. Never try to "wing it" in the virtual classroom. If you do, your mind will have to work harder to figure out what you might do next.

I'm not advocating that you should have every word memorized or read directly from a script. Instead, you should know your content well so that it's not a stumbling block when facilitating. The more familiar you are with your content, the easier it will be for you to speak while focusing on other things.

Many years ago, in my first professional job as a computer software trainer, I was scheduled to teach a one-day advanced database programming class. I had prepared for the class and felt mostly comfortable with all of the content, except for one exercise near the end of class. I had a few unanswered questions about it, but was busy and did not take the time to research them before the day of class. I planned to use my lunch break to review that section of my notes and get clarity on the activity.

Class began and went well until lunchtime. When we broke for lunch, I discovered an unexpected mandatory meeting had been called, which meant I would not have any time during the lunch break to review my notes. I was in big trouble! I returned to the classroom for the afternoon, dreading that upcoming exercise. When we got to the activity, every ounce of my attention was on following the trainer guide and my notes. Had any questions arisen, or anything unexpected occurred, I would not have been able to easily handle them.

Fortunately, this situation turned out OK. We made it through the activity, and although I felt stressed out, I don't think my students knew it. It was a huge learning experience for me. I learned to never rely on class time for preparation time, and to spend as much time as needed to prepare ahead of class.

The situation also helped me realize the relationship between a trainer's comfort with the material and his or her ability to multitask in the classroom. When you know your content, you will be able to focus on the entire scope of class instead of needing to concentrate on your uncertainties.

Know Your Virtual Classroom Software. You should be so familiar with the virtual classroom software that you can click without thinking. You should also be able to click and talk at the same time. You should know where to find every menu command, every button, and every feature of the software.

If you have to stop and think about the program features, you will not be able to effectively multitask. If you're fumbling to open the correct poll, or struggling to remember which button starts the breakout groups, you will need to focus on those things in addition to everything else you're trying to juggle.

When asked to provide his advice on multitasking, Mike Abrams, CEO of Resulting Idea, LLC, said "the biggest failure of online trainers is just not knowing the tool." In fact, Mike's secret to multitasking when delivering is "to know your tool well enough so that you can do things without thinking about it too hard." For more information about the common features of virtual classroom software, review chapter 4.

Have a Producer or Co-facilitator. When you work together with another person to facilitate a virtual class, the tasks can be divided up between you. If you have a producer, he or she can administer the technology and prepare the software tools while you focus only on delivering the content. Or, if you have a co-facilitator, you will be able to share responsibilities. Either way will free up some of your time in the classroom and allow you to more easily multitask.

It will be important to very clearly delineate roles and responsibilities so that you do not stumble over one another during delivery. There's a fine line between complementing one another and bumping into each other. Your interactions and transitions should appear seamless to the participants.

For example, if one person is responsible for monitoring the chat window for incoming participant questions, decide ahead of time if the speaker will be interrupted to respond immediately to the question, or if the speaker will take the initiative to periodically pause and ask what questions have come into the chat window. Either way is fine—you just want to work this out ahead of time. When you work together with a well-thought-out plan, you can focus on what matters most.

In one of my frequently taught virtual classes, I co-facilitate with a subject matter expert (SME). My role is to produce and to facilitate activities, and the SME's role is to present the content. The SME stays focused on his expertise: imparting knowledge to the learners and responding to questions. Meanwhile, I am able to stay focused on the mechanics of the software tool and to ensure that participants stay actively engaged. We practiced several times before our first delivery and created a comfort level working together. We are both more effective multitaskers because of our shared duties.

Be a Proficient Typist. Typing skills are necessary in the virtual classroom, especially when you use the whiteboard, the text annotation tool, and the chat window (see Figure 6–1). The better your typing skills, the better you will be able to use these tools and, in turn, the better you will be able to lead a virtual class.

Also, if you can type without having to think too much, you will be a better multitasker because your mind will not have to be focused on where to find each letter on the keyboard. Personally, I have trouble typing and speaking at the same time. Even though I can type quickly, I get tripped up if I'm typing one thing and saying another. So I've learned to either stay silent a moment while I type, or to say what I'm typing aloud.

Lengthy silence leads to disengaged participants, so speed is also important when you need to pause while typing something on the screen. When it makes sense to narrate what you are typing, such as when using the text annotation tool to type participant names for breakout groups on a slide, say their names aloud as you enter each one. This keeps them engaged while you are multitasking.

Figure 6–1. Text Annotation Sample in Adobe Acrobat Connect Pro

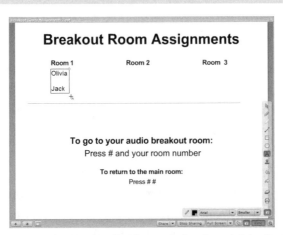

Source: Adobe® product screenshot reprinted with permission from Adobe Systems Incorporated

Remember, you need to be able to type both quickly and accurately in order to type well. They are both important, because if you type quickly but with errors, you may need to spend time fixing your typing mistakes.

Build In Pauses to Regroup. Another way to handle the demands of multitasking while delivering virtually is to build pauses into the class design. This is obviously easier to do if you have a hand in creating the class, however it can be done anytime through proper advance preparation.

Before class, review your notes to find specific opportunities for what I call a "trainer pause." These pauses are the times when you are still facilitating, but less actively engaged with the participants. Of course, there's never a time when you should be completely disengaged during class. Instead, these pauses are pockets of time when the participants are engrossed in something and you are able to briefly step back from the class.

For example, you might have a pause when

- ▶ the groups are working on an activity
- ▶ your co-facilitator is leading
- ▶ everyone is watching a video
- ▶ participants are assigned individual reflection time.

As you'll notice, these pauses are not long breaks. Instead, they are just a few moments here and there that give you an opportunity to turn to your next page of notes, take a sip of water, or mentally regroup. The short pauses give you time to recuperate and get centered, which will in turn help you catch up on whatever is needed. When you have trainer pauses during a class, you will be able to multitask more effectively.

For example, I deliver a virtual class that has a breakout group activity near the end of it. I place the participants into specific groups based upon their responses to a previous class discussion. I could create the group assignments "on the fly" right before the activity begins, but I prefer to deliberately think about who will be in each group. At one point during class, prior to the breakout groups, we have a short time of silence (approximately three minutes) for an individual reflection activity. During this time, I quickly jot down the breakout group assignments. Of course, I am not completely disengaged from the class. I'm still keeping an eye on the time and on the chat window for incoming comments, and thinking about what I'm going to say next. However, while the participants are focused on something else, I am able to catch my breath and take care of this task. When I create the breakout assignments during this trainer pause, I have one less thing to do when setting up the activity. During a trainer pause, ensure you stay close to the class, periodically speaking or typing in the chat window. If there is complete silence and stillness for too long, the participants may worry whether they (or you) have been disconnected.

Wendy Gates Corbett lets participants know when she is going to mute her phone during an activity, but that she is still available if they have questions. Then, every 30–60 seconds, she lets them know either verbally or via chat that she's still there and able to respond to questions. This gives her a moment of pause, while still staying connected to the class.

Even though planning for trainer pauses will help you multitask, it's important to remember that you won't be able to always rely on these times for a pause. If participants have a question, or a technical issue arises, your trainer pause might be filled with activity instead. While you may or may not be able to rely on having them, it's good to plan ahead and take advantage of the opportunity when possible.

Practice Multitasking. You've heard the phrase "practice makes perfect." And practicing does lead to improved performance. The more you multitask, the better at it you will be. One aspect of practicing is facilitating in the virtual classroom. As we discuss in chapter 9, you should practice virtual delivery as much as you can.

You can also practice multitasking in other situations, such as your everyday work on the computer. If you are accustomed to having just one file or software application open, try opening several at a time and switching back and forth between them while you work, practice instant messaging with multiple colleagues at the same time, or start using your software in "split screen" mode (a command that allows you to see different parts of the same file on the screen at the same time). See Figure 6–2 for a sample split screen.

When you practice multitasking on the computer in your day-to-day work, it may feel awkward at first, but it will help you get accustomed to having more than one screen open at the same time, which is typical in the virtual classroom.

Remember How You Do It in the Face-to-Face Classroom. If you're still concerned about getting used to multitasking, remember that trainers multitask in the regular face-to-face classroom as well.

Classroom trainers are like ducks on a pond—ducks look smooth as they glide along the water, but underneath the surface they are paddling like crazy just to move forward. Effective trainers make it look easy as they guide participants from one learning activity to another. Yet underneath they are working hard to keep the class moving.

Trainers look at their notes, facilitate discussion, keep an eye on the time, think about what's coming next, pay attention to participants' expressions and body language, show visual aids, and so on. Experienced trainers do these things seamlessly, without "breaking a sweat." It's just part of what they do to lead a class.

Along the same lines, effective virtual trainers make it look easy as they guide participants, even though they are multitasking behind the scenes to move the class forward. Be encouraged by your classroom experience with multitasking, because those skills can be brought with you to the online environment.

Resist Temptation to Do Too Much. Returning to our driving analogy, it's also possible while driving to add in extemporaneous activities, such as talking on a cell phone or reading a map or fiddling with the radio dials. Of course these things are not recommended, yet many drivers do them anyway.

Figure 6–2. Sample Split Screen with Two Microsoft Office Excel Files and One Microsoft Office Word File Open

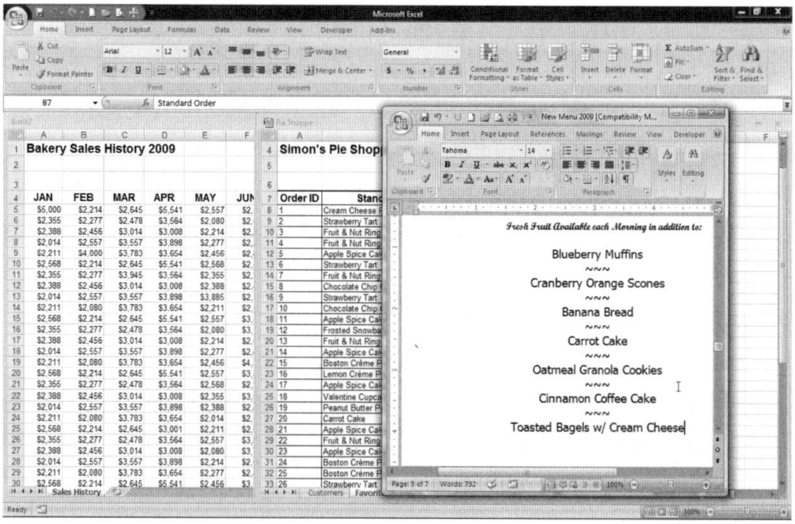

Source: Used with permission from Microsoft®

When delivering a virtual class, it might be tempting to add in extracurricular activities, such as keeping an eye on your own email or running your favorite Internet application in the background, but just like in driving, these activities pull your focus away from where it should be and could be an accident waiting to happen. It takes discipline and self-control to keep your eyes on the road in both environments.

Before your training class begins, exit out of your email program and any other instant messaging or Internet software that may be running. Close anything on your computer and remove everything from your workspace that you will not be using in class. Give your class your undivided attention. There will be enough going on in the training without adding more tasks or distractions to your virtual plate.

Know What's OK to Let Slide. Jim Wilcox, Regional Training Manager at AchieveGlobal, says his advice for new virtual trainers comes from his juggling skills.

In the book *Juggling for the Complete Klutz* by John Cassidy, the very first page directs the reader to take their juggling items, throw them up in the air, and let them drop without trying to catch them. The goal is to help the juggler get used to this feeling because that's what happens when juggling—things drop.

The same is true in the virtual classroom. Things drop through the cracks. The key is knowing what is OK to let slide, and what is not. For example, if you tell participants to raise their hands when they have a question or comment, then you don't want to miss seeing someone's raised hand (see Figure 6–3). If you do miss it, you could recover by saying, "I'm sorry, Kathy. I just noticed your hand was raised. What question do you have?"

On the other hand, if you ask all participants to respond to a question by typing in the chat window, and the responses come pouring in, you do not have to comment on each one. You can selectively pick and choose individual comments to point out during the debrief discussion. Then, at a later point in class, you can scroll through the chat window to see what you missed.

Figure 6–3. Hand Raised in Adobe Acrobat Connect Pro

Source: Adobe® product screenshot reprinted with permission from Adobe Systems Incorporated

Noted

The first secret to multitasking while delivering is to know your tool well enough that you can do things without thinking about it too hard . . . . The second secret is to use good facilitation techniques. If you need to focus on something else for a moment, do it when they are working on an activity. Ask a question and have someone answer it while you do whatever else you need to do. Don't let them know you are multitasking unless you absolutely have to. If you have to tell them, don't worry about it. They know you have many things to juggle.

—Mike Abrams, CEO, Resulting Idea, LLC

Getting It Done

You may notice a common thread among most of these tips for multitasking: Almost all of them involve advance preparation and knowledge. The more prepared you are, the easier it will be for you to deal with whatever comes your way in the classroom. Worksheet 6–1 will help you assess how prepared you are to multitask while delivering virtual training.

Worksheet 6–1: Multitasking Checklist

Use this worksheet to rate yourself on the 10 steps for multitasking success.

	Never	Rarely	Sometimes	Usually	Always
I set myself up for success before the virtual training event.	1	2	3	4	5
I am completely prepared to deliver my training content.	1	2	3	4	5
I fully know the virtual classroom software that I will be using.	1	2	3	4	5
I have a producer or co-facilitator who will assist me during the event.	1	2	3	4	5
I can type quickly and accurately.	1	2	3	4	5
I have predefined trainer pauses identified.	1	2	3	4	5
I practice multitasking.	1	2	3	4	5
I am comfortable with my virtual training delivery skills.	1	2	3	4	5
I have eliminated all distractions from my workspace in order to focus on the virtual training event.	1	2	3	4	5
I am comfortable with letting unimportant things "slide" without comment in the virtual classroom.	1	2	3	4	5

What skills are already your areas of strength?

_____

What skill(s) will you focus on first to help you be a better multitasker when delivering in the virtual classroom?

_____

Harness Your Voice

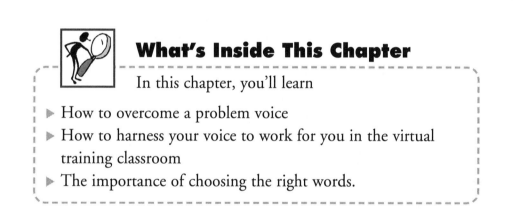

What's Inside This Chapter

In this chapter, you'll learn

▶ How to overcome a problem voice
▶ How to harness your voice to work for you in the virtual training classroom
▶ The importance of choosing the right words.

The trainer's voice can make or break the virtual training experience for a participant. Just like an athlete's ability is judged on his or her event showing, or a musician's talent shines during a performance, the trainer's voice demonstrates his or her presentation skills. It reveals the trainer's personality, interest in the topic, and it can betray his or her nervousness.

A well-known Pittsburgh sports broadcaster named Myron Cope earned fame through his unique sounding voice. He delivered one of his catchphrases, "This is Myron Cope on Sports" with emphasis on each syllable, and his distinct sound made him one of the most recognizable voices on sport radio. Some listeners loved it; others did not. Some people tuned in just to hear his funny catchphrases and unique cadence. Others avoided his broadcasts altogether.

Many people equate virtual training delivery to broadcast radio. While there are many parallels between the two, one thing is certain—trainers do not want to have a controversial voice in the training room. While everyone's voice is unique, you want to ensure it doesn't get in the way of the training. Participants shouldn't be distracted by your voice.

Your voice should be crisp, easy to understand, without annoying habits, and as neutral sounding as possible. It should allow the focus to stay on the learning—and not on your voice.

Noted

Pay strong attention to your voice.

—Jim Wilcox, Regional Training Manager, AchieveGlobal

Overcoming a Problem Voice

You might think you weren't born with a great speaking voice or you are vocally challenged. As for my voice, I have a slight lisp. I've had it my whole life, and am slightly embarrassed by it. As a professional speaker and trainer, I recognize how important my voice is to my "product." Yet I never apologize for my lisp. It's part of my personality, my style, and who I am. No one has ever mentioned it after a class, and, in fact, I'm often complimented on my voice after a virtual delivery.

If your voice is truly a challenge, vocal training is available. You could hire a voice coach or take voice lessons. Personally, I took speech classes as a child, which gave me greater control over my lisp. At times, I still follow the vocal exercises taught by my teacher as warm up before a training event.

The bottom line is that your voice doesn't have to be perfect. It just needs to not be in the way.

Watch Your Volume. When delivering in the virtual classroom, use your normal speaking voice. It's not necessary to shout. If you do, you will strain your vocal cords. You will also create sound distortion over the phone.

Think About This

Trainers frequently ask if they should use a cell phone or regular telephone for virtual classes and whether or not to use a headset or mouthpiece. The answer depends upon the quality of connection you have with either one. I recommend using the device that gives you the clearest sound. I also recommend using a high-quality wired headset so that your hands are free and there is no danger of wireless interference on the line. Also, do not try to use a speakerphone because they may sound "hollow" or have a distracting echo. Speakerphones also magnify *all* sounds, not just your voice.

In addition, some conference call providers allow you to adjust your volume as part of the participant controls. On the conference calling system I use most frequently, I can press *5 on my telephone keypad to increase my volume or *8 to decrease it.

In most cases, you will be speaking into a telephone handset or using a hands-free headset. Adjust your volume using the controls found on both the telephone and the headset (if you use one). If you are using a corded headset, make sure it's connected properly with all cords completely plugged in. If you use a wireless headset, make sure the wireless does not cause any interference or create static on the line. Place the headset microphone at a comfortable distance from your mouth.

Think About This

Speaking of volume, it is OK to ask participants to speak louder if you cannot hear them. Phrase it in a neutral-sounding way so that they don't get embarrassed (such as, "Jane, I'm having trouble hearing you. Could you please speak up?" or "Jason, we're having trouble understanding you. Can the volume on your phone be adjusted?").

Adjust Your Speaking Rate. Another common question is, "How quickly should you speak during virtual delivery?" You should speak fast enough so the participants don't get bored, yet slow enough that they understand.

Our typical speaking rate varies based on many factors. Some people naturally speak fast; others speak at a slower rate. We may speak faster when we are nervous, and slower when we are tired or not excited about the material.

According to the Lynn K. Wells book, *The Articulate Voice,* the average suggested speaking rate is 140–175 words per minute in normal conversation. You can figure out your normal rate of speech by taping yourself, listening to the recording, and counting the number of words spoken in a minute.

I'm a fast talker, and have timed myself speaking about 175 words per minute, which is on the fast edge of normal. Therefore, in both the regular training room and the virtual classroom, I make a point to slow down and pause between phrases. If I think I'm talking too slow, then I'm probably speaking at just the right rate.

Wendy Gates Corbett, on the other hand, reminds herself to speed up when delivering in the online classroom. She says that in the face-to-face classroom she speaks slower, but, together with her hand gestures, her participants stay engaged. However, in the virtual classroom, she knows she needs to speak faster, and thinks if she's talking too fast then she's probably speaking at just the right rate.

In addition to the above guidelines, ask your participants to give you feedback on your rate of speech (see Figure 7–1). You can do this live during class. Some virtual classroom software programs give participants the ability to provide real-time feedback by selecting buttons such as "speed up" or "slow down." If your software has this capability, you should encourage its use. Otherwise, ask participants for direct feedback on your speaking rate.

Additional factors that affect your desired rate of speech are the audience and your content. Keep in mind that if you have an international audience or participants who do not speak your language, you will want to talk even slower for comprehension, around 120–130 words per minute.

If you're reading from a facilitator script, you will probably speak slower than normal because your mind has to process the words on the page and then say them. Therefore, I recommend that if you have a scripted guide, you only loosely follow it. You can do this by highlighting key words, which will help you say the script, but in your own speaking style and conversational tone. You can also do this by thinking about what you're saying while you're saying it.

Figure 7–1. Sample Feedback Options for Participants in Adobe Acrobat Connect Pro

Source: Adobe® product screenshot reprinted with permission from Adobe Systems Incorporated

Keep Participants Tuned In. It's also important to be mindful of the pitch and tone of your voice when you deliver. One of the worst things a trainer can do in the virtual classroom is to speak in a monotone voice. Participants will have trouble listening to you and will not stay engaged. They will tune out. And once they tune out, it's difficult, if not impossible, to get them tuned in again!

Instead, use inflections to add interest to your voice. You can add emphasis to certain words, expressing excitement and emotion. You should sound energetic and animated about the content. How will your participants get excited about something if you don't sound enthusiastic about it? However, be careful not to lift your voice at the end of every sentence, as some presenters do, or it will sound like everything you say is a question.

Wendy Gates Corbett recommends recording one of your virtual training sessions so that you can personally hear your own voice. She did this several years ago, and said, "It was painful to hear myself—I sounded monotone and boring!" She now makes a point to intentionally modulate her voice, change her tone, and use a wider range of high and low pitch while speaking.

Keep your audience engaged with the sound of your voice. Avoid monotone speaking at all costs.

Basic Rule 12

Your voice is a key component of your virtual training delivery. Pay attention to your volume, rate, tone, and overall sound.

Minimize Your Airtime. The AchieveGlobal Adult Learning Techniques course (www.achieveglobal.com) teaches trainers to have a ratio of 40 percent airtime, giving 60 percent of airtime to the participants. This means that if you count up all of the spoken words during a class, the balance should tip toward the participants. This fact is true in both the face-to-face and virtual classrooms. The learners should be actively talking and participating in the class.

Even though you are the trainer, host, and facilitator, remember the goal is to engage your participants. Give them opportunities to speak as much as possible. Let them talk much more than you do. As we'll learn in chapter 8, asking questions, encouraging discussion, having volunteers read aloud, and so on, are all ways to keep your own airtime to a minimum.

Control Breathing. Speaking of airtime, how much air do you have in your voice? If you expel too much air when speaking, you will sound breathy and possibly hoarse. You'll need to inhale more often to keep up with your oxygen needs. Hearing you gasp for air is not attractive to your listeners. It will detract from the learning experience.

One technique for discovering how much breath in your voice is to place your finger across your lips while speaking in a normal conversational tone. Then do it while whispering. Notice the difference between the two experiences. You should feel some air on your finger while talking, but not nearly as much as when you whisper.

If you find yourself gasping for air while speaking, familiarize yourself with deep breathing techniques, which will help improve your lung capacity. Deep breathing will also help you stay calm and collected in a nervous situation.

When I need to take a deep breath, I do so by inhaling as much as I can through my nose, holding a moment, and then exhaling through my mouth. Another deep breathing technique I use is to put my hand on my abdomen while breathing, which helps me breathe deep into the belly instead of taking shallow, chest-only breaths.

Take a few deep breaths before you begin class, and then again as needed during class.

Posture Affects Your Voice. Sit? Stand? Kneel? How do you position your body when delivering in the virtual classroom? Believe it or not, your posture affects the way your voice sounds.

In my first job as a corporate trainer, I was taught to always stand and never sit during class. I've since relaxed this rule, because sometimes a seated facilitator encourages more discussion, especially in smaller classes.

Similarly, when I first started virtual training, I always stayed seated and fixed to my chair during class. It just seemed natural to do so. However, I've since adjusted this rule because sometimes a standing trainer has more energy in his or her voice. If I use the hands-free headset, place my laptop on a stand, and arrange my notes in an easy-to-see location, I can facilitate a virtual class on my feet.

There are obviously times I do stay seated throughout the entire virtual class. But now I'm much more open to varying my posture than before. You might do the same—experiment with various options to find the best one for you.

When sitting, sit on the edge of your seat, and sit straight up with your head over your shoulders and your shoulders over your hips. Not only does sitting with proper posture make it easier to breathe properly, it will also help you sound more energetic and engaging. If you slouch in your chair, or lean back with your feet up on the desk, you might sound too relaxed and nonchalant. It may only result in a slight difference in your tone, yet your demeanor will translate across the phone line.

A final thought about posture: Smile while you speak. Your smile can be "heard" by your participants, and it adds energy to your voice.

Control the Nervous Voice. When I get nervous, you can hear it in my voice. That may be true for you as well. Your voice can betray you when you are nervous. Nerves can be heard when your voice shakes, or when you speak too quickly, or when your voice squeaks in a higher pitch.

You can keep shakiness from your voice by using deep breathing techniques and ensuring you are prepared. And, as discussed previously, you can control your rate of speech. However, it's harder to control your voice range when it rises because of nerves. Jim Wilcox suggests maintaining your "morning voice" when you know that nerves may get the best of you that day.

Your "morning voice" is how you speak when you first wake up in the morning. For most of us, it's in a lower tone than our usual voice. You can work to keep your voice in that register range by keeping your vocal cords in that range right from the start of the day. For example, hum in that same low voice while you are in the shower. On your drive to work, listen to the radio and repeat the newscaster's words aloud or sing along to the music. All the while, remain in that lower register of your morning voice. Continue to hum softly until class time. Then, when class starts, if you get nervous and your voice rises, it will simply rise to your normal register instead of going too high. Your nerves will be masked!

Warming Up Your Voice. In general, warming up your voice is another important preparation technique for trainers. If you've ever tried to speak on a moment's notice and been caught with a "frog" in your throat, then you understand the importance of doing this. When your voice is already warmed up, your voice will not crack when you begin speaking.

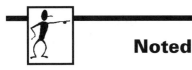

Noted

Make sure that a morning training class is not your first conversation of the day. Try warming up your voice by talking to someone ahead of time, either in person or on the telephone.
—Sharon Wingron, Founder and President, Wings of Success, LLC

Several of my training colleagues recommend using techniques from singers and professional broadcasters who warm up their voice by repeating phrases or singing scales ("do-re-mi"). Jim's recommendation on how to keep your vocal cords warm is to hum in a low register, just below audible level, for a few minutes before speaking. He says it's just the act of getting air past your vocal cords that keeps them warm.

Noted

Repeat the phrase "red leather yellow leather" while doing scales. Start from low notes to high notes singing this over and over. Once you are at the top of your good sounding scale, come back down. Then try to do it a bit quicker. This is a great way to warm up your face, lips, mouth, and throat.

—Mike Abrams, CEO, Resulting Idea, LLC

Stay Hydrated. To help your throat stay hydrated when delivering virtual training, have room temperature water available to you throughout the session. I recommend room temperature because water that's too hot or too cold can affect your vocal cords.

In addition, water is a better choice than other beverages for several reasons. Carbonated sodas will cause unpleasant effects from their effervescence. Caffeine is a diuretic, which will make you need to visit the bathroom. Milk and other dairy-based beverages will coat your vocal cords, which could make you sound congested.

If you have a glass of water, put a lid on it so it doesn't accidentally spill. If you use bottled water, crack open the top before the session so that you don't need to fumble with it during class. Also, don't use a straw, since that increases the air intake to your digestive system and could result in an unwanted belch during class.

Recently, I was facilitating a virtual class and accidentally knocked over my full water cup. As water spilled across the desk, I quickly picked up my laptop and set it on a nearby table. I scooped up my wet notes and put them on my chair. I reached for napkins to start sopping up the water, and kept on going. At my next opportunity, I ran to get a towel (wearing my telephone headset) to clean up the rest of the spilled water. My participants never knew what happened. But I learned the lesson to always have a covered lid on my water glass.

Choose the Right Words

While we're on the topic of voice, let's also talk about what you say. Specifically, the words you choose to use.

First, deliberately choose words that evoke emotion and add interest to the topic. For example, you could say, "wow, this is cool" or "an exciting new way to do this is . . . ." Of course, use phrases that are genuine to your personality and speaking style. Wendy Gates Corbett, provides software training in the virtual classroom, and she uses phrases like, "I'm excited about this feature" or "My favorite topic is . . . ." These add interest and convey her enthusiasm about the program.

Second, be careful about using phrases that not everyone will understand. These phrases to avoid include idioms, colloquialisms, and slang. For example, if you're used to saying, "This is a piece of cake," you can instead say "This is easy." Instead of saying, "The ball is in your court," you could say "That's your decision." Be mindful of the phrases you use in your everyday language that might not translate well in the virtual classroom. Another virtual trainer I know once used the phrase, "Don't throw the baby out with the bathwater." One of her international participants had to stop her and ask, "What do you mean?" The class ended up laughing about the experience; however, it's good to be careful of our word choices!

Third, avoid gobbledygook. Gobbledygook occurs when you use extra words to communicate or when you use larger words than needed. Just like we're taught to avoid wordy phrases in written communications, we can avoid gobbledygook in our speech. For example, say "use" instead of "utilize" or "try" instead of "attempt." Keep your word choices simple.

Carefully choose your words so that you are clear, concise, and perfectly understood by your listeners.

Avoid Filler Words. Sometimes we say words without consciously realizing it. Words like "um," "OK," and "y'know" creep into our voice. Everyone else hears them but us. Wendy calls these words "verbal viruses" because they are easy to catch and hard to eliminate.

We all have filler words that we naturally gravitate toward using. Mine is the classic "um" between sentences. I also say "absolutely" much more often than anyone should.

What's yours? If you don't know, ask someone who knows you well. They will probably be able to tell you immediately. You could also call yourself and leave a voicemail, reminding yourself to complete an upcoming task. Then during playback, you'll hear your filler word of choice.

The harder question is how to eliminate your filler word. The first step is to recognize you have one and to identify what it is. The second step is to start listening for it when you talk. And the third step is to consciously stop saying it. You might pinch yourself every time you use it or keep a hash-mark tally count when you hear it. One preventive measure I've used is to write the filler word on a sticky note, and then place the note in an obvious spot.

You may have more than one filler word that you use. If so, repeat the above steps for each one. Also, once you've stopped saying a filler word, the trick is to not replace it with another one. Instead, eliminate it altogether. Be OK with a silent pause, and don't feel like you have to fill that space.

Reduce Self-Talk. The other words you should eliminate are what I call your "trainer self-talk." Trainer self-talk happens when you think out loud—talking to yourself about what you're doing or mistakes you've made.

In the face-to-face classroom, trainer self-talk can be eliminated by simply not saying anything to draw attention to small mishaps. For example, if you thumb through a flipchart pad looking for the correct page, and while doing so say, "It's taking me a while to find the right page," that's an example of trainer self-talk. Your participants probably would not have noticed that it took you a few extra moments to land on the right one, but since you told them, they are now thinking about the extra time. The alternative is to simply thumb through the chart without drawing attention to the few extra moments it takes you to find the correct spot.

It's a similar situation in the virtual classroom. Let's say you accidentally highlight the wrong word with the annotation tool. You could mention your mistake, or you could just use the annotation eraser tool to remove the highlight. If you do the latter, most participants won't notice the minor error you just made.

For example, you might say, "Oops, I didn't meant to click on that" or "My connection is slow today." The self-talk occurs when you point out to your audience something that they did not need to know. There's no need to call attention to your mistakes. Most of the time, especially if you quickly recover, your participants will not notice the error.

It's a delicate balance between telling participants what you're doing for them on their behalf versus pointing out mistakes, delays, or technical glitches. For instance, it would be appropriate to say out loud, "In a moment we will take a poll, which I am opening now to display on your screen," or, if you need a moment of silence to create online breakout groups, you could say, "It will take me just a moment to assign you to your groups." These statements are helpful and add value to the participant experience.

In the virtual classroom, there can be a very fine line between what you should and should not share aloud. Keep the hidden things hidden.

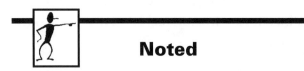

Noted

I plan how to use my voice. What I mean is, when I practice, I actually make notes like "slow down here" or "emphasize this—speak louder." . . . I have to use my voice as a major delivery tool.

—Kathy Shurte, Manager Training Development and
Performance Management, Florida Department of Transportation, District 4

Getting It Done

Your voice communicates who you are as a virtual trainer. Make your voice work for you. Learn to control your voice. Exude energy and excitement through it. Convey to your participants your personality through what you say and how you say it. Use your voice to effectively deliver the virtual training.

Worksheet 7–1 contains techniques to warm up your voice before delivering a virtual training event.

Worksheet 7–1: Vocal Warm-Up Exercises

Select one or more of these techniques to warm up your voice prior to delivering a virtual training event.

1. Quietly hum your favorite song.

2. Slowly say the alphabet vowels (a-e-i-o-u). Exaggerate your facial expressions while doing so. Repeat in various vocal tones (low, medium, high) and in various volumes (soft, medium, loud).

3. Sing the musical scale (do, re, mi, fa, so, la, ti, do) forward and backward several times in a row.

4. Open your mouth as wide as you can and say "ahhh" (as if you were in the dentist chair). Close your mouth, and then repeat.

5. Warm up your facial muscles by pursing your lips together (like a kiss) and then smile wide. Go back and forth between these mouth positions.

6. Warm up your neck muscles by gently looking side to side, and then up and down.

8

Engage Participants

What's Inside This Chapter

In this chapter, you'll learn

▶ How to effectively engage participants
▶ How to keep training relevant and bring it to life
▶ The importance of capturing participants' attention from the start
▶ To focus on the learners.

In a *T+D* article, synchronous learning expert and author Jennifer Hofmann wrote, "Teaching online is like teaching after lunch." In case you're not familiar with the post-lunch phenomenon, classroom trainers jokingly refer to it as the "teflon hour" because "nothing sticks." It's a challenge at this time of the day to keep participants' attention and to engage them in the class.

In the virtual classroom, the problem of engaging participants is even more pronounced. Some would say this is the fundamental challenge of virtual training—how to effectively engage participants and keep their attention throughout the class.

There are several reasons for this challenge. First, participants usually do not leave their personal workspace to attend synchronous online training. Instead they stay in their own environment, which means they see their "to-do" lists, their files, and their pile of unfinished work. In addition, they may have pop-up calendar reminders that interrupt the session, or even that little yellow "unread email" icon in the corner of their screen. All of these things are hard to ignore as they silently beckon to the participant throughout the virtual class.

Second, some learners might be new to the virtual classroom and may not realize that you expect them to actually participate. Their previous experience may have been with webcasts or other noninteractive online sessions. These false expectations just create more obstacles for a virtual trainer to overcome.

Also, this 90-minute virtual session could be the only block of time that day when participants' telephones don't ring or they are not interrupted. Therefore, they may see it as "down time" and want to take advantage of the opportunity to catch up on other things. In these days of perpetual connectivity, even if participants shut down their email programs, they can still use their smartphone to read and respond to messages during the class. In fact, in some business cultures, they might even be expected to do so.

Participants may also think they *can* successfully multitask during your training class. Even if they stay engaged for most of the session, they assume it won't matter if they take a few moments to quickly respond to an incoming email message or to rearrange the items on their desk.

I actually find this challenge to be an interesting paradox. As a virtual trainer, you need to multitask and pay attention to many things at once. Multitasking is both expected and needed for the trainer to be successful. Yet we ask participants *not* to multitask. We ask participants to keep their sole attention on the virtual classroom.

Let's face it—it *is* difficult for participants to have a singular focus. It *is* difficult for many participants to break their habit of multitasking, especially when they stay in their own work environment to attend the training. And it *is* difficult for participants to ignore the temptation to do other things in the midst of the training class.

Therefore, to help participants stay focused on the virtual classroom, trainers need to keep participants engaged throughout the entire event. The good news is that this can be done, and it can be done successfully. An effective virtual trainer with a well-designed course *can* maintain the attention of participants. Effective trainers encourage participants to multitask, but within the boundaries of the intended learning activities. Also, effective trainers keep the training pace brisk, give frequent opportunities to interact, and offer multiple options to engage.

Noted

Remember it is still about involving your participants and staying focused on their learning. It is not about just getting through content.

—Sharon Wingron, Founder and President, Wings of Success, LLC

Effectively Engaging Participants

Let's look at eight ways to effectively engage participants:

- Make it matter.
- Keep it relevant.
- Capture their attention from the start.
- Say participants' names frequently.
- Create interactivity using technology.
- Encourage networking.
- Bring the training to life.
- Focus on the learners.

Make it Matter. To effectively engage participants in the virtual classroom, you need to "make it matter." This means you appeal to participants' internal motivations by showing them the "WIIFM" ("what's in it for me?"). This also means you help the learners see the benefits of participating in the class. If the learning outcomes of your virtual training course are important to the participants, then they will be much more likely to engage in it. You, the trainer, can help them see how the training matters to them.

To do this, begin with finding out the big picture of the training initiative. You may already know it if you were involved with the design of the program. If not, seek out someone familiar with the training and ask appropriate questions, such as

- What is the overall purpose of this training?
- What do the learners need to know as a result of attending?
- To what business or performance results will they be held accountable?
- What are the potential consequences if the learners don't learn?

You should ask these questions ahead of time so you know what will motivate the participants. Knowing the overall purpose of the training will help you put this specific topic into context. Knowing what the learners need to know as a result of attending will help you stay focused on that outcome. And knowing what business or performance results are needed will help you help them achieve those expectations.

When you know the answers to these questions, it will help you clearly articulate the training class' benefits to the learner. You'll be able to show them the "WIIFM" from their perspective. You can emphasize this information throughout the session at appropriate times. When participants realize the training will benefit them, their internal motivation to learn increases, and they will stay more engaged in the class.

It's possible that you could discover there are no answers to these questions. In other words, it may be an unfortunate situation where the training class is not tied to business results or does not have performance-based learning objectives. It may simply be a "nice-to-know" topic or awareness-building session. Or, you may have been brought in just to facilitate the class, without any available insight into the before-or-after implementation. In this case, do everything you can to help participants see how this content matters to them. Ask them to share what *they* want to learn, and how this learning will benefit them.

Another way to "make it matter" is to encourage management involvement before and after the class. If the participants' direct supervisors talk with them beforehand about the importance of the training, then the learner will be more likely to actively engage in the class. Do what you can to influence these conversations ahead of time. If you're able, send a note to the managers and let them know their involvement is important. Personally call the managers and ask them to get involved. Offer to hold a virtual session just for them, to expose them to the training material (if they're not already involved with the training initiative). Or, at the very least, include them on pre-event communications.

When you "make it matter," the participants will be more inclined to stay tuned into the class.

For example, in a sales training program I deliver, we begin class by asking participants to list specific challenges they personally experience during sales calls. Then throughout the class, I refer back to the personal challenges listed and tie our lessons to them. These connections help participants see the benefits of each learning objective.

Three ways to show WIIFM ("what's in it for me?"):

▶ Emphasize benefits by reviewing each item on the class agenda with a comment related to how it will help them.

▶ Ask the participants to share how they expect the training topic to benefit them.

▶ Collect class alumni testimonials and share those comments with the class.

Keep It Relevant. Virtual trainers should keep the class focused on content that is interesting, relevant, and immediately applicable. The best-case scenario is that the training class design makes this easy. In the worst-case scenario, the trainer has to work harder to make this happen. When trainers keep the class relevant to the participants' real-world environment, the learners will be much more likely to stay engaged.

"How can trainers do this?" you might ask. "If the trainer follows the facilitator script, won't it automatically lead to the learning outcomes regardless of its relevancy to the participants?"

Well, not exactly. Trainers add their own style when facilitating a class. They add stories and examples to enhance the content. They ask impromptu questions to generate discussion and to follow up on participant comments. These enhancements are a normal part of most training classes.

It's like ballroom dancing. A dance, such as the waltz or tango, is immediately recognizable because it follows a set of rules. However, each couple on the dance floor looks different because of how they interpret the dance. You would know two people are dancing the waltz, but because of their personal style, they may look altogether different than the couple next to them.

It's the same with training. Two trainers could deliver a class using the exact same facilitator script, and you would recognize the class, but each trainer's individual style would be obvious. When a trainer injects his or her own style into the class, the discussions will be unique to that session. The stories told, the examples shared, and the emphasis on certain components all will be distinctive to the trainer leading the class.

Therefore, when you deliver virtual training, keep your stories and examples relevant to the class. You could share how the current lesson relates to your six-year-old's funny comment last week, or you could share how the current lesson relates to a common business challenge. Both stories may illustrate the learning point; however, you should share the one that your participants will relate to most. In fact, you could compile several stories or examples to use in each class and then select the one most appropriate for your audience that day. These stories will add your unique style into the training while still maintaining participants' interest.

For example, I recently co-facilitated a financial-related virtual training class. During the class, my co-facilitator shared examples of where to find companies' publically available financial information. He ensured that every example was relevant to the participants because he listened to their introductions and comments about the companies they work with. When it came time to share the examples, he could have used a set of preplanned generic company names. Instead, he deliberately used the companies that participants had named during the session. He not only used those specific names, in some cases he referred to their websites. In fact, every time we run this class, he tailors the examples to the participants in attendance. It helps because when they hear the company names they work with every day, they pay closer attention.

In another virtual class I frequently facilitate, we discuss the challenges of coaching. To give participants an example of the type of challenges we'll be discussing, I share a short story about a coaching dilemma I encountered as a new supervisor. It's a story that is relevant to both the topic and the audience, and it helps illustrate the discussion point.

Think About This

You don't have to be the only storyteller. Everyone has a story. Encourage your participants to share their own examples and stories. If a participant goes off-topic or shares what seems to be a nonrelevant example, gently ask him or her to link it back to the training topic. For example, in a listening effectiveness course, you could say, "Oliver, thanks for sharing. That's an interesting example. What aspect of it could best help everyone remember how to listen effectively?"

Virtual trainers should do everything they can to keep their stories, examples, and discussions relevant to the participants. The more relevant the material, the easier it is for participants to stay engaged.

Noted

My favorite tip is to tell stories. . . . People relate to stories; they will engage and remember your presentation. It's very cool to be sharing a story, and seeing things like, "Wow! I didn't know that!" appear in the chat box.

—Kathy Shurte, Manager, Training Development and
Performance Management, Florida Department of Transportation, District 4

Capture Their Attention From the Start. Begin engaging your participants even before the official start of class. Participants are usually encouraged to log in to the virtual classroom early, and many of them do. Unfortunately, in many virtual sessions, this time is not used. This time before class is usually just a time of silence while everyone gets connected. Sometimes a participant needs technical assistance, and this time is used to help them. Frequently, the producer or trainer simply greets the participants and lets them know, "We'll begin at the top of the hour."

In order to capture participants' attention from the start of their experience, get them engaged from the moment they log in. Use this otherwise "dead time" to get the participants involved and excited about the class. When you capture participants' attention right away, you will be like a conductor leading orchestra warm-ups, or like a coach leading athletes in calisthenics prior to a game.

To understand why it's important to get participants involved from the start, imagine a virtual class from their perspective. Let's say the class begins at 10 a.m. Joe Participant logs in to the virtual classroom at 9:50, and sees a screen that says, "Class will begin at 10 a.m." So, Joe thinks, "I have 10 minutes . . . great! I can get a few more things crossed off my to-do list!" And then he starts reading and responding to email. He is still logged in to the virtual classroom, but at 10 a.m. when class starts, he may be in the middle of responding to one last email and therefore not ready to begin.

Instead, if you have something for the participants to do once they log in to the virtual classroom, you will be more likely to keep their attention once the class starts. This initial activity helps transition participants from work to the class. In some ways, it allows participants to ease into the class gradually instead of having a "hard" start time.

This pre-class activity should get them involved yet it should not be a complete lesson of critical importance to the learning outcomes. The goal is not to begin class too soon. You don't want to penalize the participants who do arrive on time but not early. Instead, this technique is more of a bonus for those who do arrive early. It serves the purpose to capture participants' attention from the start.

There are a number of things you can do during this time of anticipation prior to class. For example, use the introductory screen to

▸ share a relevant quote and ask participants to comment on it in the chat window

▸ post part of an interesting statistic about the topic and ask participants to guess the correct number

▸ have a poll question open and ask participants to respond to it

▸ invite participants to share their expectations for the class, either verbally or in the chat window

▸ ask participants to comment on any pre-class assignments.

When you engage participants from the time they log in to the virtual classroom, they will be more likely to stay involved during class. It helps them know that this class will be interactive, and they are expected to participate.

Figure 8–1. Sample Pre-Class Activity Slide in Adobe Acrobat Connect Pro

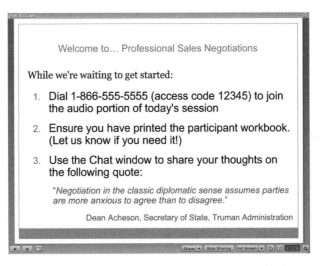

Source: Adobe® product screenshot reprinted with permission from Adobe Systems Incorporated

In addition to this pre-class activity, reinforce this message of interactivity by giving participants something to do within the first five minutes of class. The last thing you want is 10–15 minutes of "introduction" time at the beginning of class. While this may be fine in a face-to-face class, it will not work in a virtual class. You need to engage the participants from the start, and keep the activity level high throughout.

Basic Rule 13

The general rule of thumb for a synchronous virtual training class is to engage participants at least every three to five minutes.

Here are just a few ideas on how to engage participants within the first few minutes of class:

▶ Have participants introduce themselves by annotating a map graphic to indicate their current location.
▶ Invite participants to say hello to the group by typing their usual greeting in the chat window.
▶ Open a whiteboard and have participants type in a question about the class topic.

Think About This

If you have an international audience that crosses multiple time zones, you could have participants type in the current time of day and current weather in the chat window. Time and weather is something we can all relate to and these questions will help personalize the people behind the names.

Finally, in chapter 2, we talked about establishing ground rules. One of the items that should be emphasized—both verbally and visually—is the expectation that this will be an interactive class. Tell them right at the start that everyone will be expected to participate. Let them know that you will call on them by name during class. Let them know that there will be activities for them to complete. Let them know that their fellow learners are counting on them to take an active role in the class. Let them know that there will be assignments and opportunities to interact. And then follow through by capturing and keeping their attention throughout class.

Say Participants' Names Frequently. People like to hear their own names. When people hear their name spoken, their ears perk up and they listen. Therefore, you should say your participants' names often throughout the training class.

There are several ways to incorporate your participants' names into the class. First, when you ask questions or expect involvement, call on people by name to respond. For example, you could ask, "Sophie, what do you think about this process?" or, "Emily, please tell us your experience in using this tool." Remember, these direct questions should be ones that have no right or wrong answer so you maintain a comfortable learning environment. The point is to encourage participation, not to embarrass or put someone on the spot.

Mike Abrams has an additional tip related to calling on people by name. He recommends warning that you will be calling on participants by name, so they will be prepared. Your warning might be telling a participant exactly what you will be asking: "Bob, I'm going to ask you to answer question five after Maria answers question four."

Another way to use participants' names in the class is to incorporate their names in your examples. For instance, you could say, "Tomorrow, when Sarah goes to use this new skill, she would first follow these steps . . . " Or, say something like, "From past experience, at least two of you will have a question about this next week. Jack might wonder about X, and Bradley will probably want to know more about Y." Using their names will both help personalize the content and help participants stay engaged.

A third way to incorporate participants' names into the class is to frequently refer back to comments they have made. You may remember that a participant asked a question or made a statement, and you can mention it again at appropriate times during class. For example, you might say, "This next topic will give us even more insight into Emma's earlier question" or, "Natalie told us about her experience with X, which also applies to this step in the process."

If you want to use this technique but are not sure that you will remember participants' comments and questions, use a blank page to make notes during discussions. Prior to my virtual classes, I print an extra copy of the roster with participants' names and keep it on my desk next to my notes. During the introductions, I jot down any pertinent comments that participants make about themselves or the class content. I continue to take short notes on this page during class, and refer back to it frequently.

The more you can use participants' names during class, the more your participants will stay engaged.

Think About This

It's not just about saying participants' names, but also how you say them. When you incorporate participants' names into your speech, use a conversational tone of voice so that it sounds genuine and not forced.

Create Interactivity Using Technology. One of my favorite benefits of delivering synchronous online classes is all of the technology available to use. Virtual classroom software programs are full of features that can make the training interactive. We reviewed these tools in chapter 4.

A well-designed virtual training class will use all of the technology tools offered by the software platform.

However, the trick to creating interactivity is to use these tools thoughtfully. Do not just use the tools just because they are there. Use them because they will engage participants, keep their attention, and move everyone toward the learning outcomes.

Your program may be interactive if it uses the technology tools to engage participants. But, it's important that every activity have instructional value leading to the intended learning outcomes. If the class *only* has interactivity, it would be just like a face-to-face class that is full of fun and games but has no learning purpose. That type of training is like cotton candy—it looks good but has no substance.

Wendy Gates Corbett, my *Infoline* co-author, recommends that trainers "change lanes" often while delivering virtually. This means that, just like drivers who frequently change lanes while driving, a virtual trainer should frequently transition between methods during class. You can do this by ensuring a good mixture of the technology tools are used to engage participants.

For example, if you have a series of questions to ask, consider having the participants respond verbally to one set of questions, and then in the chat window for the next set of questions. If you want the participants to brainstorm, have them use a whiteboard the first time, and then the chat window the second time.

You can also "change lanes" beyond the technology through your facilitation. For example, if you call on participants by name to respond, use various methods to do so. The first time you call on participants, you might ask them to use the "raise hand" button. The next time you call on participants, start with whomever is dialing in from the farthest time zone and then work your way around the globe. The next time, go in reverse alphabetical order.

I once had a virtual participant named Anissa who logged in to the classroom as "Nissa." When she introduced herself as Anissa, I asked her which name she preferred to be called. She replied "Anissa," but then went on to explain that she deliberately signed in as "Nissa" because in a previous class, the trainer always called on her first to respond because her name was at the top of the list.

See Table 8–1 for ideas on how to use the tools to engage participants. There are several other books and resources that give activity ideas using a virtual classroom's technology tools. See the resources section for more information.

Encourage Networking. In a face-to-face class, learners naturally interact with one another and the trainer. Even if they are shy to participate, they may speak to the person sitting next to them or interact with others during small group activities. However, learners in a virtual classroom often perceive the social element to be missing and are less likely to engage with others.

For many, the virtual classroom seems like an anonymous environment. Therefore, they may remain hidden during class. Since participants do not leave their personal workspaces to attend class, and do not see their fellow classmates, they may feel alone. The result of feeling alone and anonymous means attendees are less inclined to get involved. Virtual trainers need to work extra hard to build rapport among participants and to promote participation.

When the trainer encourages networking, they get the participants involved with each other and therefore engaged in the class. Virtual trainers should strive to create

Table 8–1. A Sampling of Engaging Activities Using Common Virtual Classroom Tools

Share Documents	Have key topic points listed on a slide. Ask participants to use the annotation tools to highlight or mark "what stands out to them." Then have the facilitator use the highlighted words as the basis for discussion.
	Write an incorrect fact on a slide. Have participants shout out what's incorrect about it, and then have them state the correct fact.
	Post a topic-related puzzle or game board on a slide (such as a crossword puzzle or hangman). Have participants use the annotation tools to play the game.
Whiteboard	Use the whiteboard to brainstorm solutions to a problem posed by the facilitator. Have the producer take notes or ask for a volunteer scribe.
	Ask participants to type on the whiteboard using the annotation tools to summarize lessons learned so far during class.
	Prepare the whiteboard with a grid and assign each participant to a specific area. Ask participants to share examples of the content by drawing a relevant symbol in their assigned area.
Polling	Ask participants to share their opinion on a topic by voting "for" or "against" it. Use the results as a discussion starter.
	Use the polling or survey tool to quiz participants on any pre-class activities. Create a friendly competition by having participants track how many questions they answered correctly.
	Check for knowledge transfer by periodically quizzing participants on the content and having the facilitator respond to the results.
Chat	Have sentence starters on a slide (For example, "I'm surprised by . . . " or "I now understand . . . "). Ask participants to complete the sentence by typing in a public chat window.
	Ask participants to discuss a topic with an assigned partner using private chat.

(*continued*)

Table 8–1. Continued	
Interactive Discussions	Give the participants a "Buzzword Bingo" game board as part of the handout package. Invite participants to play along during the class, listening for key words related to the training topic. Invite participants to call out "bingo" as appropriate.
	Ask participants to provide feedback during a mini-lecture by using the virtual classroom's raise hand or change status feature.
	Have a printed handout with fill-in-the-blank spaces. Ask participants to complete the handout during the discussion.
Multimedia	"What's the next line?"—play short audio clips of a conversation and ask participants to tell you what the next line should be. (For example, if the class topic is how to provide feedback, the conversation would be a feedback dialogue.)
	When showing a video, provide a video observation form in the handout so that participants can take notes while watching.

Adapted from *Infoline* No. 250911, "Designing for the Virtual Classroom," by Wendy Gates Corbett and Cindy Huggett.

a shared learning experience among participants. One subtle way to do this is to use inclusive language when speaking, such as, "*We* will cover X in today's class," or "*Let's all* turn to page three of the handout." Another subtle way to do this is to allow participants to see the attendee list. (Some virtual classroom programs have the ability to show or hide the list, so make sure it is visible to all.)

In addition, trainers should always take time to do some type of participant introduction activity. If the class size is small, participants could take turns introducing themselves. If the class size is large, then participants could all type an introduction in the chat window or annotate one on the screen. It's important for participants to see and hear the other learners in order for them to feel more comfortable engaging with the group.

My favorite way to engage participants through networking is to assign participants to a team and have them work together on class activities. An obvious way to work in teams is to use the virtual classroom software's breakout group functionality. Less obvious but still effective ways include

▸ Have a friendly team competition for points. Assign point values to questions, and the first person to answer a question wins points for their team.

▸ Create two-person teams and allow them to communicate with each other via private chat. Give team assignments and have each pair report back.

Any opportunity you can use to get participants networking with each other, do it. It will not only add a social element to the learning, it will help you engage participants and keep their attention.

Bring the Training to Life. Trainers who communicate using more than words are more likely to engage participants throughout the class. For example, a trainer could simply tell everyone the four steps to a decision-making process. Or, a trainer could display a visual aid that matches the four steps, use the four steps in a recognizable example, and offer an acronym to aid memorization. A trainer could also tell a story about the four steps and use an analogy to help participants understand them. All of these methods are examples of bringing the training to life, and each one will help engage the participant by offering an interesting and memorable class.

Wendy Gates Corbett frequently uses this technique to engage participants. In one of her virtual classes, she posts a picture of a box with "fragile" stamped on it and asks, "How many of you have purchased a new computer?" She then goes on to discuss with participants the set-up process for a new computer and relates it to an administrative set-up process that they'll be learning in the class. Her visual depiction of a new computer puts the image in participants' minds and helps them put the training topic into context.

In another class, Wendy creates a word picture using serving dishes as an example to explain how to distribute content in a learning management system. She relates the distribution process to someone who needs to serve food, and who has a choice over what type of serving dishes (big plates, little plates, bowls, cups, and so on) to use based on the type of food they are serving. This simple yet powerful analogy brings the training to life by using an everyday example that is easily relatable.

Wendy's technique engages participants by giving them a visual hook—something to think about to help them learn the training content. The visual hook helps keep them involved in the class.

You can (and should) use this technique. As part of your pre-class preparation process, plan ways you can bring the training to life. Think of analogies and word pictures you can use to help explain the concepts. Through your word pictures, try to engage participants' senses—sight, smell, sound, touch, and taste. The more you appeal to the learners, the more likely they will be to pay attention while you are speaking.

Focus on the Learners. The last tip to engage your participants may be the most important. Effective virtual trainers always remember that the focus is on the participants, and not on the trainer. It's not about us—it's about the participants and their learning.

For example, a coach on a sports team usually has one goal: to help the team win a championship. The coach's decisions throughout the season reflect this goal. The coach keeps the focus on the players and helps the team play its best. It's the same in your virtual classes. Your goal is to help participants learn.

Many years ago, as a young training professional, I attended an ASTD International Conference & Exposition session led by train-the-trainer expert Bob Pike. He talked about the difference between being a "Sage on the Stage" versus a "Guide on the Side." He said that a great trainer puts the participants at the center of the experience. The entire class is about the participants instead of the trainer. The trainer's role is simply to guide participants along to achieve intended learning outcomes.

I have found this advice to be true in the virtual classroom as well. When trainers focus on themselves, participants tune out. When trainers focus on the participants, they are more likely to stay engaged.

One way to show your participant-centric focus is to make deliberate yet subtle word choices. Instead of saying, "I want you to turn to page four" or "I will now cover the next topic," you might say, "Let's all turn to page four" or "We will now review the next topic." These are minor semantic changes, yet they reveal who you are focused on. Participants pick up on these slight differences (if only subconsciously), and that helps keep them engaged.

Another way virtual trainers can guide participants through the learning is to ask a lot of questions. Questions elicit responses from participants, which in turn keeps them actively involved. We have already discussed effective questioning techniques in chapter 2, including how to provoke discussion, be specific, and maintain a comfortable environment. When you apply those facilitation techniques, they will help keep participants engaged in the class.

Noted

Ask questions and wait for multiple answers. Ask questions that elicit a story, not just a yes or no. Don't be afraid of white space (the empty space where no one is talking). It's OK to put pressure on your participants to fill the nervous gap of silence. When you think it's time to continue as the silence has gone on long enough, count to five. You will be surprised who responds in that last few seconds who would not have shared before.

—Mike Abrams, CEO, Resulting Idea, LLC

Getting It Done

Keeping participants engaged may be the biggest challenge of virtual training. It is challenging to do for many reasons. However, with a good class design, and excellent facilitation skills, a virtual trainer can successfully engage participants during the entire session. Worksheet 8–1 will help you prepare before class to engage participants.

Worksheet 8–1: Engagement Worksheet

Use this worksheet to help you engage participants during class.

Name of training class: _____

Part 1: Purpose

What is the overall purpose of this class?

_____

What do the learners need to know as a result of attending?

_____

To what business or performance results will the learners be held accountable?

_____

What are the potential consequences if the learners don't learn?

_____

Part 2: Class Preparation

Based on the answers to the previous questions, what can you specifically do or say to help learners see the benefits of participating in the class?

_____

_____

What relevant stories and examples will you share during class?

_____

_____

How can you capture their attention from the moment they log in? What activity or exercise can they do prior to class?

_____

_____

What word pictures or other visuals can you use to bring the training class "to life"?

_____

_____

9

Practice, Practice, Practice

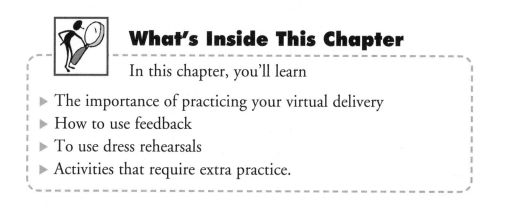

What's Inside This Chapter

In this chapter, you'll learn

▶ The importance of practicing your virtual delivery
▶ How to use feedback
▶ To use dress rehearsals
▶ Activities that require extra practice.

What do world-class athletes and musicians have in common? They spend hours and hours each day practicing. Musicians do warm-up exercises, practice basic techniques, and play musical pieces over and over again. Prior to a public performance, they do a complete dress rehearsal to ensure all of their show components are ready.

Athletes also practice regularly. They practice basic skills, run drills, and simulate game-day situations. Depending upon the sport, they may practice with the rest of their team or they may practice on their own. They work with a coach who sees an alternate perspective on their performance. And they use their practice time to get physically and mentally prepared for the next exhibition.

Practice Makes Perfect

Virtual trainers need to do exactly the same: practice, practice, practice. Trainers should practice both on their own and with others. Trainers should practice their basic virtual delivery skills. Trainers should simulate the online classroom environment when practicing, and run through "drills" to prepare for every scenario. Trainers could also work with a "coach," who will see a different perspective on their classroom performance.

Many years ago when I was a training manager, the trainers on my team would be scheduled for a few days of prep time before each new class so that they could learn and practice the material. Each one had his or her own preparation style. One trainer in particular would go into an empty classroom and practice facilitating a class from start to finish. She pretended to have an audience, and walked through every activity as if people were participating. At the time, I thought that type of thorough rehearsal was overkill; however, I now believe that it is exactly the right thing to do for virtual classes. You should have at least one, and preferably more, complete dress rehearsal of the virtual training session.

All trainers, regardless of experience or skill level, should take time to practice delivering virtually. Even if you can think fast on your feet when facilitating, practicing is still critical to your success. You may be able to "wing it" in a face-to-face class with successful results. But spontaneously delivering a virtual class simply will not work. In the physical classroom, you could stumble over a few words when speaking yet make up for it by your smile, gestures, and overall appearance. However, in the virtual classroom, when you stumble over your words, it sounds as if you are not prepared.

Noted

My advice for new virtual trainers? Practice as though you were actually doing it, and do it more than one time. Practice changing slides. Practice using the whiteboard. Practice opening polls. Play around with it, and get comfortable with it. Practice everything.

—Tracy Stallard, Training Performance Consultant, AchieveGlobal

We have already talked about preparation in chapter 5. This chapter, on the other hand, focuses specifically on how to practice your virtual delivery. We'll look at ways to set up a practice environment, and how to complete a full dry run of your virtual event.

Noted

An extemporaneous introduction in the face-to-face classroom may sound OK. Yet saying exactly the same words in the virtual classroom could sound sloppy and unprepared.
—Joe Willmore, President and Founder, Willmore Consulting Group

You can maximize your training effectiveness through quality practice. When you practice virtual delivery techniques, it improves your overall facilitation skills. When you practice using the virtual classroom software, it improves your ability to multitask and to successfully deliver training in this environment. And when you practice using the content, it improves your knowledge of the topic and ability to check for learning transfer.

Whether this is your first or 100th virtual delivery, practicing your techniques will improve your skills. Think of it this way: even Super Bowl champions, Stanley Cup winners, and World Series victors go back to basic training camp at the beginning of each season. They practice the fundamentals to improve their performance. So should virtual trainers.

General Practice

If you are new to virtual delivery, begin with general practice sessions. Look for opportunities to lead virtual meetings or to give short online presentations. You could do this within your organization at internal meetings or offer to help with someone else's virtual class.

One way to practice delivering is to partner with colleagues who are proficient in the virtual classroom. Ask if you can co-facilitate a class with them. They may be willing to share the stage, or at least help you get started with some practice.

For example, one of my colleagues was asked to deliver a virtual class. She had no online training experience, so I worked with her to help her learn. We made arrangements to co-facilitate the first few classes together. In addition to our other preparation steps, we practiced the full session together three times before the first delivery. The practice opportunities both helped her get comfortable with the online classroom and allowed us to rehearse our handoffs and division of responsibilities.

There are also plenty of places to practice if you want to start somewhere other than work. Look for local volunteer opportunities, especially with groups who meet virtually. As a training professional, get involved with your local ASTD chapter. Many chapters hold virtual meetings, and if you volunteer for the program committee or a leadership role, you will most likely have an opportunity to practice your virtual delivery skills.

If you want to get started on your practice but do not have easy access to a virtual classroom software platform, take advantage of the free trial accounts available through most vendor websites. Create your own online events, and invite friends or co-workers to participate.

Jeff Smith, Senior Consultant with The Titan Group, was an early adopter of virtual technologies. However, he started small and practiced. His first sessions were not with clients. Instead, he started using the technology in a "low-stress" environment—internal department meetings. He and his team began playing around and experimenting with the tools. They gave presentations, used the software tools, and practiced. This helped them learn and get comfortable with virtual delivery. The more they practiced, the better they became.

When you practice, focus on getting comfortable with the technology and delivering to an audience you cannot see. This is your opportunity to try things out and play with the software. You can practice multitasking—looking at your delivery notes while keeping an eye on the chat window and other screen elements. Practice as often as you can and more than you think you need.

If you are an experienced virtual trainer, use this practice time to take your "game" to the next level. Focus on the small nuances that can have big impact on your delivery. For example, are you using inclusive language ("let's all look at this model") instead of trainer-centric language ("I want you to look at this model")? Or, notice if you have eliminated all of your filler words from your delivery. Although I don't recommend recording live training events, this is one time a recorded session could be useful. When practicing for delivery, record the session and then play it back to critique yourself and identify areas for improvement.

Think About This

Pay special attention to one technique at a time when practicing your virtual delivery. For example, one time you might focus on your rate of speech, and the next time give extra attention to your word choices. While it's important to have the complete delivery package, during your practices you can strive for improvement in one area at a time.

Getting Feedback

When you first learn how to deliver virtually, invite people you know and trust to be your participants in general practice sessions. Ask them to honestly evaluate your delivery, and be open to their comments. Solicit feedback on the following elements of your delivery:

- ▶ voice (is it clear? easy to hear? good tone and pitch?)
- ▶ word choices (any filler words? unnecessary trainer self-talk?)
- ▶ rate of speech (too fast? too slow? just right?)
- ▶ activity instructions (clear, concise, and complete?).

When gathering feedback on your practice, ask participants to share one thing you did well and one suggestion for improvement. Or, ask each person to focus on one of the above items and provide specific positive and constructive feedback on just that area. What's important when receiving feedback is to listen without getting defensive and to be open to ideas for change.

Dress Rehearsals

Just like Broadway shows and other live performances hold dress rehearsals, your virtual training events should also have dress rehearsals.

The first time you deliver each new virtual training class, plan to walk through it in full as if you were delivering it. That means if it is a 90-minute session, you would have at least a 90-minute rehearsal. If you have a producer or any co-facilitators, they should also participate just as they would during the live training event.

Plan to run at least two full dress rehearsals prior to delivering a virtual class for the first time. The first dress rehearsal will help you test the technology and flow of activities. The second dress rehearsal will reinforce your preparation and allow you to check any changes that were made after the first rehearsal.

Basic Rule 14

Schedule dress rehearsals far enough in advance of the training so there is time to make necessary changes to the class and, if needed, time for additional practice.

Dress Rehearsal Environment. You will want to set up your dress rehearsal practice environment exactly the same as you would to deliver the class. This means you will

- prepare your trainer notes and all class files
- set up your personal workspace with your primary computer and a sidekick
- set up the virtual classroom as if you were expecting your participants to arrive
- set up the same telephony options that you plan to use during your event
- invite mock participants to attend the session.

During a dress rehearsal, it's important to always use the exact virtual classroom software that you will be using for your class. Recently, I worked with a trainer who was delivering in the virtual classroom for the first time. My role for the event was to be the producer, and she would be the main facilitator. We initially practiced using the virtual training software, which in our case was hosted by a third-party vendor. We also used the third party's conference calling system for our audio connection. We then practiced using the client's version of the same virtual training software and their conference calling system, which were both hosted by a *different* third-party vendor. In our dress rehearsals, we noticed a few small differences between the systems, such as the telephone moderator commands and the default participant privileges. While these differences may seem insignificant, they could have had a big impact during the virtual event if we were not aware of them.

Dress Rehearsal Participants. Ideally, the participants you invite to the dress rehearsal will not know the content or be familiar with the course design. This will more realistically mimic the class.

It's also good to have the instructional designer and other trainers participate in the dress rehearsal. They can give you feedback from their perspective on the flow and timing of activities, as well as tips for improving your virtual delivery skills. They'll also be able to keep an eye on the participant involvement and whether or not the overall class outcomes are met as intended.

If for any reason (availability, confidentiality of the content, and so on) you have trouble finding available practice participants, don't let a lack of people prevent you from holding a dress rehearsal. You could invite friends or family who know nothing about the virtual classroom to log in and act as participants. Or, at the very least, you could set up multiple computers in your own work environment and pretend to have participants—just like my classroom trainer did years ago.

If possible, have your dress rehearsal participants use the same types of computers that the real participants will be using. This includes various operating systems, browsers, and screen resolutions. It may also include different Internet connection speeds. This variety will help you authentically replicate the class environment.

Think About This

It's important to test out a variety of connection options to the virtual classroom software during a dress rehearsal. You might discover that your visual aids do not show well on a particular monitor resolution, or that the video playback in one location is problematic. Discovering these unexpected abnormalities prior to the training event will give you time to troubleshoot and correct the issues.

When conducting a second or third dress rehearsal, invite new participants to attend. There is an advantage to having the same participants attend each rehearsal—

they can give you feedback on what improved from the first session. However, in order to fully practice in a realistic training environment, you should have participants who are not familiar with the material attend each time. A compromise would be to have a mixture of "old" and "new" participants in each rehearsal, which could give you the benefit of both scenarios.

Things to Look for During a Dress Rehearsal. When you facilitate a dress rehearsal for a new virtual training class, there are several things to look for during the delivery:

▶ Activity choice: Is this the best activity for the learning outcome? Does it engage participants?

▶ Activity flow: How well do the activities flow from one to the next? Are they in the best order?

▶ Activity transitions: Are the transitions between activities smooth and seamless?

▶ Instructions/directions: Do the participants know exactly what they should be doing at all times? Are any additional directions needed?

▶ Visual aids: Do the visual aids (such as Microsoft Office PowerPoint slides, whiteboards, and handouts) match the course content?

▶ Timing: How does actual timing compare to the expected timing? What activities need more time? Less time?

▶ Speaker transitions: If more than one person is delivering (co-facilitators and/or a producer), are the transitions between speakers smooth and seamless?

If your dress rehearsal reveals significant design flaws or major changes to be made, be open to these changes. This is one reason the dress rehearsal should be scheduled far enough in advance of the first delivery—so that changes can be made.

In the case of a virtual class that has been delivered many times and tested by other trainers, your focus should be less on the activity design and more on your own personal delivery of it. The questions above are still valid; you simply consider the questions in a different context. For example, if during your dress rehearsal the timing of an activity was way off the intended time, consider how your delivery can be adjusted to make the allotted time work. If participants were not clear on the instructions for an activity, review the word choices you used when giving those directions. Or, if the visual aids did not match up, was it because you forgot to change from one slide to the next?

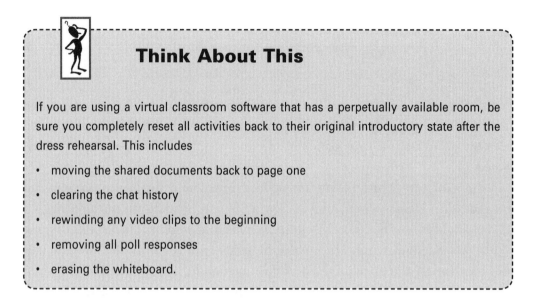

Think About This

If you are using a virtual classroom software that has a perpetually available room, be sure you completely reset all activities back to their original introductory state after the dress rehearsal. This includes

- moving the shared documents back to page one
- clearing the chat history
- rewinding any video clips to the beginning
- removing all poll responses
- erasing the whiteboard.

Tips to Remember for Timing. Just like in a face-to-face class, your timing may not go as planned. The discussion could go off on a tangent or you could have someone who talks too much. You may also have more participants than you expect, which makes some activities take longer.

Therefore, during your practice, determine content areas that could be shortened without detracting from the learning objectives of the class. For example, if you would normally ask for four volunteers to share a personal example, you could ask for only two volunteers to share. Or there might be a "nice to know" activity that the participants could do on their own after class.

The opposite holds true, of course. In the rare instance where you find yourself with more time than needed, you could give your participants the gift of this extra time and release them from class early, or you could consider which activities could be expanded. These additions should enhance the learning experience and not just "fill time" for the sake of making class last longer.

Activities That Require Extra or Special Practice

In some cases, an activity looks good on paper but falls flat in the online environment, or the technology does not work as you expected. In addition, it's important to know what you, as the trainer, should see and experience during the activities and what the participants should experience during the activities. Pay special attention to the following activity types and software features during your practice sessions.

Polls. Determine at what exact point a poll question needs to be opened. If you are co-facilitating or working with a producer, figure out which one of you will open the poll to solicit participant answers, and when and if the poll results will be shared.

In one of my virtual classes, my co-facilitator and I discovered an awkward moment when loading a particular poll question. The handoff was not smooth, and we had dead time in the class. Therefore, we practiced working out the exact timing of our poll question setup. Now, when he lands on a certain slide, I briefly take presenter control and open up the next poll question behind the scenes. I then turn presenter control back over to him before he needs it. Later in the class, when the poll question is needed, it's already loaded and just needs to be opened for participant responses. The participants are unaware of our handoff, and the awkward moment no longer occurs.

Whiteboards. Practice annotating and typing on the screen, and then erasing. Look to see if everything shows up exactly as expected, both for you and for the participants.

In one virtual classroom software I use, I discovered that one of the annotation tools shows up slightly to the right of where I click, instead of on center. I also discovered that the default highlighter color did not show well on my slide background. I was able to make adjustments prior to the class to accommodate for these tools.

Breakout Groups. Determine how you will assign participants to a breakout group, and exactly when you will release them to their groups. Notice if there will be any lag time between the activity directions and the start of the breakout group. Also determine if any before-class breakout room preparation needs to be done by the trainer, and, if so, how and when you will do it. In addition, plan what you will do during the breakout group activity—will you go in and out of the rooms or stay in the main room? If you visit the rooms, will you be a silent observer or speak to the group? Will you communicate with the groups in the midst of the activity or let them work on their own?

When I practice assigning breakout groups, I like to plan ahead of time who will go into what groups. I consciously assign partners and teams to promote networking across departments and locations. I also test out the frequency of communicating with the groups during an activity. I don't want them to be interrupted by my intrusions, yet I also don't want them to be lost without direction. During practice, I try to determine the appropriate amount of facilitator involvement in each breakout group activity.

Shared Web Browser. Practice transitioning to the website you wish to view during class. This transition should be as seamless as possible to the participants. For example, have your webpage preloaded or saved as a quick link so you can jump right to it without stopping on your browser's default home page. Also, if you plan to type in any fields or dialogue boxes that remember your previous entries, clear out your browsing history and Google searches—otherwise participants might see your past websites and searches. Make it as "clean" as possible for the participants.

I once watched a trainer share his web browser, and start typing in a search window. His browser settings caused past searches to appear on a drop-down list as he typed, which is usually a helpful shortcut for Internet searching. While there was nothing unusual about his past Internet searches, he paused for a moment when the auto-complete list appeared. It's always a good idea to clear your history prior to a virtual delivery, just in case.

Here's an example of what all this practicing and rehearsing looks like in real life: One of my clients had the same virtual training class scheduled eight times over a five-month timeframe. Prior to our first delivery, my co-facilitators and I held four dress rehearsals. Then, immediately after each class, we met to debrief the experience and make all necessary adjustments to our materials. I also reset my facilitator notes and the virtual classroom materials. Then, a few days before the next event, we would each individually review and prepare for the upcoming class.

Getting It Done

The more you deliver in the virtual classroom, the more practice you will get and the better your training will be. If you are an occasional virtual trainer, make a deliberate choice to schedule practice time in your calendar before every event. The conscious decision to continually practice your delivery will reduce your anxiety and improve your classes. Even if you practice frequently, remember that this practice does not take the place of your class setup (see chapter 5). Instead, this practice is in addition to it.

Also remember that regardless of how often you deliver the same virtual class, it's a good idea to consider each session as a practice dress rehearsal. Solicit feedback after each class, making notes about what can be improved about your delivery. Feedback is a gift when you are open to it. Use your practice time to improve your training. Use Worksheets 9–1 and 9–2 to track your practice sessions.

Worksheet 9–1: Practice Checklist

Use this checklist during a dress rehearsal for a virtual training class.

Topic	Questions to Ask	Changes to Make for Next Time
Activity choice	• Is this the best activity for the learning outcome?	
Activity flow	• How well do the activities flow from one to the next?	
Activity transitions	• Are the transitions between activities smooth and seamless?	
Instructions/ Directions	• Do the participants know exactly what they should be doing at all times? • Are any additional directions needed?	
Visual aids	• Do the visual aids (slides, whiteboards, handouts, and so on) match the course content?	
Timing	• How does actual timing compare to the expected timing? • What activities need more time? Less time?	
Speaker transitions	• If more than one person is delivering (co-facilitators and/or a producer), are the transitions between speakers smooth and seamless?	

Worksheet 9–2: Practice Schedule

Use this checklist to track your practice sessions.

Name of training class: _____

Facilitator name: _____

Co-facilitator name (if applicable): _____

Producer name (if applicable): _____

Date	Time	Participants	Feedback Received	Action Items

10

Know What to Do When Everything Goes Wrong

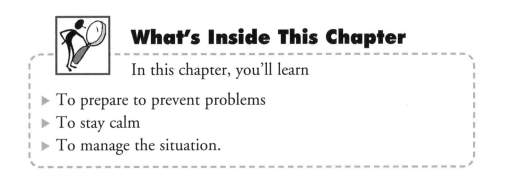

What's Inside This Chapter

In this chapter, you'll learn

- ▶ To prepare to prevent problems
- ▶ To stay calm
- ▶ To manage the situation.

Virtual training classes often have challenging moments. From technology problems to connection issues to unexpected glitches, all of these conditions are common in synchronous online events. Many trainers fear this aspect of virtual training. They are concerned about how to handle the problems and what to do when things go wrong.

Yet it's not much different from the problem-solving skills trainers use in the face-to-face classroom. In the classroom, trainers deal with challenges all the time—broken projectors, missing materials, video players that don't work, distracting noise, and other unexpected commotions. When these things happen, skilled classroom trainers simply manage the situation and move on with class.

It's the same in the virtual classroom. Things can and will go wrong. You will encounter everything from participants who cannot connect to a software feature not working as planned to unexpected disruptions to the class. All of these and more are typical occurrences during a synchronous online event. When these things happen, skilled virtual trainers simply manage the problem and move on with class.

There are three rules to follow to keep your problems and their impact to a minimum:

1. Prepare to prevent problems.
2. Stay calm.
3. Manage the situation.

Let's explore each one in detail.

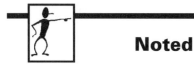

Noted

Expect something to go wrong.

—Jim Wilcox, Regional Training Manager, AchieveGlobal

Prepare to Prevent Problems

The number one thing you can do when things go wrong is to be prepared.

Your preparation before a virtual training class begins can literally make or break the event when something unexpected happens. Your preparation makes it easier to deal with technical glitches and problems. Your preparation also helps you handle participant issues. The more prepared you are, the easier it will be to respond when things don't go as planned.

For example, if your class includes a video, then your preparation could include uploading the video script to the virtual classroom software's file sharing tool. Then if the video playback experiences unforeseen problems, participants will have easy access to the script and you could ask for volunteers to act out the dialogue. Or, if your computer crashes unexpectedly but you have prepared a second back-up computer, then you could quickly switch to it while continuing class. Or, if you prepare extra slides with activity instructions, participants who may not have printed the handout will still be able to engage. Each of these situations could be a disaster that affects the virtual class, yet your advance preparation prevents disruption.

In another example, trainer Jeff Smith was delivering a virtual session when his co-facilitator had to make an early exit due to a fire in her building. Jeff had to deliver the rest of the class on his own. He was able to do this because he had prepared both sections of class—just in case. When the "just in case" became the case, he was able to stay calm and continue the class, without negatively affecting the participants.

Noted

Everything is dependent on how well you prepare ahead of time.
—Tracy Stallard, Training Performance Consultant, AchieveGlobal

In essence, the main purpose of this book is to prepare you to effectively deliver virtual training classes. If you have completed all of the recommended actions up to this point, then responding to problems during a virtual class should not be a big deal. By following the steps you will have

- ▶ learned about technology
- ▶ mastered the virtual classroom software program
- ▶ set up for success
- ▶ improved your ability to multitask
- ▶ harnessed your voice
- ▶ practiced over and over again.

The probability of something going wrong in the first place will diminish if you have fully followed all of these steps. When something unexpected *does* happen, you will be able to rely on your knowledge of the technology, the virtual classroom software program, and contingency plans you have prepared. You'll keep your voice calm, and you'll be able to multitask by keeping the class going while dealing with the situation.

For a few examples of how your preparation can help you respond to a problem in the virtual classroom, see Table 10–1.

Table 10–1. Preparing for Problems

Situation	Possible cause	A step you take during preparation to prevent the situation	A possible in-the-moment response
A participant has trouble logging in to the virtual classroom event	User error if the participant does not have the correct web link or types in the wrong password	• Ensure participants have correct connection information prior to the class • Have both the host/trainer link and password and the participant link and password in an easily accessible spot	• Email the correct link and password to the participant • Verbally tell the participant the link and password information
A virtual classroom software feature does not work as planned (such as a poll question does not load)	User error if the producer or trainer clicks on the wrong button	• Master the virtual classroom software program, knowing all of the buttons and features • Practice all the software features ahead of time	• Pause, then click on the correct button • Switch to a contingency plan, such as typing the poll question on the whiteboard
Participants are not able to annotate on the screen or whiteboard	User error if the producer or trainer did not enable this participant functionality	• Practice all the software features ahead of time • Follow all pre-class set-up procedures, including checking required participant privileges	• Navigate to the participant privileges screen and enable these privileges

There are times when you will be fully prepared yet things will still go wrong, such as a server outage or unanticipated disaster. Despite your best efforts, these unexpected occurrences could create problems for your virtual training class.

For instance, another trainer and I recently delivered a series of virtual training events for an organization. We had practiced and prepared, and separately delivered several successful sessions. Then one day, for some seemingly unexplained reason, my training colleague began a class and nothing seemed to work. Several participants had trouble logging in to the session. Others were able to log in but were not able to see the shared document. Still others were not able to see the video clip during the class. The trainer did everything she could to prepare yet these problems still occurred. Later, we found out that the participants' IT department had made some organization-wide technology updates on everyone's computer, and had not thought about how this would affect our training. We were not aware of the updates. This lack of communication, coupled with the technology changes, created a difficult situation for the virtual event. The trainer had to deal with these unexpected challenges. Luckily, she was able to do so, in part, because she stayed calm, which leads us to the next technique for handling challenging situation.

Stay Calm

When things go wrong, the key is to stay calm. Take a deep breath. Pause, so that you can think clearly enough to react appropriately. Assess the situation and decide what to do next.

It's the mark of a professional in any field to remain cool and collected under stress. Effective virtual trainers do so as well. They maintain their composure and stay calm when things go wrong.

Noted

The more you call attention to a technical glitch, the more people will focus on it. Instead, recognize it, manage it, deal with it, and move on.

—Tracy Stallard, Training Performance Consultant, AchieveGlobal

For example, if a software feature is not working the way you expected it to, and you have a contingency plan for the activity, you could simply go to the alternate activity without mentioning it to the participants (such as, "Let's respond to this next question via the chat window"). Or, if you had already told them to expect a poll and you have to change to a contingency plan, just do it without giving too much extra detail (such as, "Instead, let's switch and respond to this next question via the chat window").

Basic Rule 15
When something unexpected occurs, take a deep breath and stay calm.

Don't be overly concerned with how participants will react when they know there is a problem. Most will work with you when things go wrong. In the face-to-face classroom, when a flipchart marker runs dry and the projector bulb blows, the participants realize these things happen and do not get upset. The classroom trainer's appropriate response to these situations is to stay calm, get another marker, or keep going without the projector until the next break. It's the same in the virtual classroom. When unexpected technical difficulties occur online, most participants are very understanding. Especially when the trainer stays calm in the situation.

Think About This

Be aware of what you say out loud when things go wrong. Be mindful of your trainer "self-talk," which may have a tendency to appear when something unexpected happens. Your initial response may be to comment on the problem, which may or may not be appropriate for the situation.

Manage the Situation
When things go wrong in the virtual classroom, you should take steps to manage the situation and keep the class going. It's best if you can maintain the flow of the class

and keep the situation seamless to the participants. Ideally, they won't even know that there is a problem. If the problem is obvious to one or more participants, then it's just a slight challenge that gets worked through without too much disruption to the learning.

For example, Jeff Smith was in the middle of leading a virtual session when something unexpected happened to his telephone connection. As a result, the participants could only hear every other word he said. Once he realized there was a problem, he simply typed a chat message to let everyone know what he was about to do, and then he hung up and dialed back in. His connection was fixed, and the class continued along as planned.

In a similar example, Jim Wilcox was co-facilitating a virtual training class. His co-facilitator was in a separate but adjoining conference room. In the middle of the session, it was Jim's turn to speak, and for some unexplained reason, his telephone remained on mute. He had pressed the right buttons but his phone remained silent. He was speaking, but no one heard him—except the co-facilitator in the adjoining room, who could hear his voice through the wall. She took over for him and facilitated his portion of the class. Eventually, he realized that no one could hear him, so he simply hung up the telephone and dialed in again. Meanwhile, it was seamless to participants, and the class continued on schedule.

Not long after one of my recent virtual classes began, the online meeting and associated conference call unexpectedly ended. I was not able to reconnect. I opened my email program, sent a quick message to all of the participants in the class, and asked them to stay tuned for directions. I then created another online event using the virtual classroom software, sent the participants a new connection link and telephone conference code, and restarted the training. It took a few minutes for me to reload the presentation materials and poll questions. We lost about 10 minutes of time, but the participants were understanding and ready to continue learning.

What's the common thread between these stories? In all cases, something unexpected happened. And in all cases, the class continued mostly as planned. The trainers stayed calm, they took steps to remedy the situation, and they managed the problem.

Which is exactly what you should do when an unexpected problem occurs during your virtual training class—manage the problem and keep the class moving forward.

Managing Technical Problems. When technical problems occur, hopefully you have a producer who can step in and troubleshoot the problem while you continue the class. This is one of the main reasons a producer is recommended. One of the producer's primary roles is to handle the technical components of the virtual class-room, which includes problem solving.

If you don't have a producer, you could ask a technical contact or a fellow trainer to join the virtual class for the first 10 minutes. Because most connection problems occur during the first few minutes of class when everyone is logging on, ask this person to be your "as-needed, short-term, back-up troubleshooter." Unless there are major problems that arise, this person is free to log out and drop off the line after the first 10 minutes of class.

There are times when it's not possible to have a producer, co-facilitator, or any additional help. In those cases, your multitasking skills are truly tested. As a general rule of thumb, if you can quickly work with an individual participant having trouble, then go ahead and do so. For example, if you can get them back on track in under a minute's time, then proceed to help them. However, if it will take you longer than a minute to help them out, consider what other options are available.

In a recent virtual class of mine where I was alone without a producer, a participant temporarily lost his Internet connection and could not find the meeting link to reconnect. He needed the specific meeting number and passcode for our session. I knew I could quickly tell him the information he needed, even faster than I could get it to him via email. So, I paused the class to verbally give him the information. It took just a moment, and everyone was understanding while he received the troubleshooting assistance needed. Had he needed more involved technical assistance, I would have offered one or two short suggestions, and then either asked him to press #0 (the operator-assistance code for my conference calling provider) or asked him to reschedule the class for another time. If he were in a building where another participant was connected, then I would have considered asking him to go pull up a chair next to that person and share a connection.

For a list of common technical problem and troubleshooting tips, see Table 10–2.

Think About This

Emphasize to participants the importance of joining class early—at least 10 minutes prior to the start time. That usually gives everyone time to deal with any unanticipated connection problems before class begins.

Table 10–2. Common Technical Problems and Troubleshooting Tips

Problem	Troubleshooting Tips
Participants can't log in	• Check the web link and passcode they are using • Have them close their browser and re-open it before trying again
Participants do not see your screen and/or shared documents	• Use the virtual classroom software's "synchronize" command to sync everyone's display • Have them exit and re-enter the virtual classroom event
Participants have trouble seeing or hearing a video clip	• Require participants to test the virtual classroom software features prior to the class • Have them check to ensure the volume is turned up • Have a printed copy of the video script available
Trainer has trouble sharing a document	• Check the file type compatibility with the virtual classroom program • Instead of sharing the document, share the application (or share your desktop with the application open on it)

Aside from connection challenges, most technical glitches are specific to the software you are using. For example, as we reviewed in chapter 4, one platform may have participant privileges that control what the participants can and cannot do in each event. Another platform may have unique rules over how the eraser works on a whiteboard. As you learn and practice the software tools, make note of how these features work so you can become an expert in troubleshooting them.

 Noted

If worse comes to worse, you can always reschedule the session. Strange things have happened and will happen. Keep a level head, make a joke, and move on.

—Jeff Smith, Senior Consultant, The Titan Group

Getting It Done

The moral of the story is to expect the unexpected. Things can and will go wrong when you are facilitating in the virtual classroom. While it's hard to predict what specifically will go wrong, you can rest assured that at least one challenging situation will probably happen during class. This fact is true for even the most prepared trainer. Therefore, remember the three steps to handle it: prepare thoroughly, stay calm, and manage the situation. By doing these, you will keep the class moving toward the learning outcomes. Use Worksheet 10–1 to keep track of problems that arise during your training classes.

Worksheet 10–1: Troubleshooting Log

Use this log to keep track of problems that arise during your training classes. Frequently refer back to this list as a learning tool.

Name of training class: _____

Name of virtual software classroom program: _____

Date	Problem Description	Troubleshooting Tips (What did you try? What worked?)

About the Author

Cindy Huggett has taught hundreds of training classes for a variety of audiences. Her participants have ranged from executives to frontline employees. She has successfully designed curriculums, facilitated classes, and led training rollouts in almost every industry and every size organization.

Cindy started her training career as a software instructor, teaching corporate clients how to use personal computers when they were new to the workplace. She's always been an early adopter of technology, and enjoys sharing her lessons learned with others.

Cindy has spent the last 18 years in various training, consulting, and learning management roles. She currently owns an independent consulting practice (www .atrainerslife.com) and is also a Training Performance Consultant with AchieveGlobal (www.achieveglobal.com).

Cindy co-authored two ASTD Press *Infolines*, "Simple, Effective Online Training" (January 2008) and "Designing for the Virtual Classroom" (November 2009). She has also contributed to the *The Trainers' Warehouse Book of Games* (Pfeiffer, 2008) and the forthcoming *The Leadership Challenge: Activities Book* (Pfeiffer, 2010).

She holds a Master's degree in Public and International Affairs from the University of Pittsburgh and a Bachelor's degree from James Madison University. Cindy was one of the first training professionals to earn the Certified Professional in Learning and Performance (CPLP) designation.

Cindy's passion in life is helping others achieve success. She has been recognized numerous times for her leadership skills and commitment to serving others. She is the past president of the ASTD Research Triangle Area Chapter and the current chairperson of ASTD's National Advisors for Chapters. Cindy connects with individuals by offering development opportunities for their personal growth. This book continues her passion to help others, with hope that classroom trainers achieve success in virtual deliveries.

Cindy lives in Raleigh, North Carolina, with her husband Bobby. You can contact her via email (chuggett@gmail.com) or find her sharing training tips on Twitter (@cindyhugg).

References

■■

This book outlines the steps to virtual training success. By following these tips and techniques, you will become more effective at delivering online training. However, your quest doesn't—and shouldn't—stop there. Due to the rapid pace of change with technology, I encourage you to continue learning about virtual classroom software programs and their evolving features. The following resources will assist you in your journey.

References and Resources

American Society for Training & Development (ASTD). *2009 State of the Industry Report.* Alexandria, VA: ASTD Press, 2010.

Beich, Elaine. *Training for Dummies.* Hoboken, NJ: Wiley, 2005.

Cassidy, John and B. C. Rimbeaux, *Juggling for the Complete Klutz.* Palo Alto, CA: Klutz Press, 1994.

Clark, Ruth Colvin and Ann Kwinn. *The New Virtual Classroom: Evidence-Based Guidelines for Synchronous e-Learning* (with CD-ROM). San Francisco, CA: Pfeiffer, 2007.

Conner, Marcia L. "Informal Learning." 1997–2009. Retrieved on September 18, 2009 from www.marciaconner.com/intros/informal.html

Corbett, Wendy Gates and Cindy Huggett. *Infoline* "Designing for the Virtual Classroom." Alexandria, VA: ASTD Press, 2009.

Hofmann, Jennifer. "Teaching Online is like Teaching After Lunch." *T+D Magazine*, January 2004, pages 19–21.

Hofmann, Jennifer. *The Synchronous Trainer's Survival Guide: Facilitating Successful Live and Online Courses, Meetings, and Events*. San Francisco, CA: Pfeiffer, 2004.

Hofmann, Jennifer. *Live and Online!* (with CD-ROM). San Francisco, CA: Pfeiffer, 2004.

Hofmann, Jennifer and Nanette Miner. *Tailored Learning: Designing the Blend that Fits*. Alexandria, VA: ASTD Press, 2009.

Huggett, Cindy and Wendy Gates Corbett. *Infoline* "Simple, Effective, Online Training." Alexandria, VA: ASTD Press, 2008.

Leonard, Karen. *The Corporate Learning Factbook 2009: Benchmarks, Trends and Analysis of the U.S. Corporate Training Market*. Oakland, CA: Bersin & Associates, 2009.

Pike, Robert. *Creative Training Techniques Handbook* (3rd ed.). Amherst, MA: HRD Press, 2003.

Shank, Patty, ed. *The Online Learning Idea Book*. San Francisco: Pfeiffer, 2007.

Wells, Lynn K. *The Articulate Voice* (3rd ed.). Needham Heights, MA: Allyn & Bacon, 1999.

Wexler, Steve. *360 Report on Synchronous Learning Systems*. 2008. Retrieved on September 18, 2009 from www.elearningguild.com

Virtual Training Seminars

AchieveGlobal (www.achieveglobal.com)

Bob Pike Group (www.bobpikegroup.com)

InSync Training (www.insynctraining.com)

Online Resources

Adobe Acrobat Connect Pro Users Group (www.connectusers.com)

eLearning Guild (www.elearningguild.com)

Learning Circuits (www.learningcircuits.org)

Select Virtual Classroom Software Vendors

Adobe Connect Pro (www.adobe.com/connect)

Cisco WebEx (www.webex.com)

Elluminate (www.elluminate.com)

GoToWebinar (www.gotowebinar.com)

Microsoft Live Meeting (www.microsoft.com/livemeeting)

Index